The Blended Learning Cookbook
Second Edition

by Clive Shepherd

Published in collaboration with Saffron Interactive

First published in the United Kingdom in 2005. This edition 2008.

ISBN number: 978-1-4709-7865-5

Design – Jenni Grove, Saffron Interactive

Contents

Preface to the Second Edition

Since we produced the first edition of the Blended Learning Cookbook, the world has changed a great deal. When we talk about 'the blend', we no longer simply mean a mix of traditional e-learning and classroom training and the concept of the stand-alone 'course' is arguably redundant.

e-Learning now offers learners sophisticated and varied options to support their learning. Meanwhile, the development of read-write technology for the web has seen the addition of wikis, blogs and social networking sites to the blend, building communities of learners and making their experience truly interactive. This, along with new ways of using video, gaming and podcasts has taken blended learning to new and exciting levels, not only forming an integral part of formal training interventions but also in supporting continuous informal learning.

In this second edition of the Cookbook, we have added new recipes and enhanced some of the existing ones to reflect the changes that these advances in technology have made possible. Like the first edition, the recipes provide practitioners with examples of outstanding successes and blueprints for best practice. This cookbook is for anyone who wishes to improve the effectiveness of their current training interventions, who wants to understand how e-learning can be integrated into a broader learning process and for anyone looking for innovative approaches to training. We hope you find these useful and that your programmes are as fun, engaging and worthwhile as the projects that form the basis of this book.

Hanif Sazen

Hanif Sazen is Chief Executive Officer of Saffron Interactive, a business communications company providing blended learning solutions to Global 500 organisations.

SAFFRON
INTERACTIVE

Gray's Inn House	Tel: 0207 092 8900
127 Clerkenwell Road	Fax: 0207 242 2757
London	cookbook@saffroninteractive.com
EC1R 5DB	www.saffroninteractive.com

Foreword to the Second Edition

Blended learning is no longer a major talking point in learning and development and perhaps that's not such a bad thing. Bandwagons are fun when they arrive in town and they certainly make some money for those selling conferences, books, magazines and consultancy; but more often than not, when they've made a lot of noise parading down the main street, they disappear off into the distance, leaving behind a whole load of headaches and hangovers. But, as ever, there's little chance of much peace and quiet, because there's always another bandwagon not far behind. In the case of blended learning, following it into town came the bandwagon snappily labelled Learning 2.0, laden with musicians trumpeting blogs, wikis and social networks.

Now, if I was cynical, I'd spot an opportunity here. After all, the Learning 2.0 bandwagon is itself losing a bit of momentum while organisations work out how on earth they put it into practice and when 'sticking to the knitting' seems to be more appropriate as we enter a recession of potentially monumental proportions. What is the opportunity? Well, it comes from the realisation that blended learning and informal learning are not actually mutually exclusive concepts; in fact I will argue that they make very compatible bed-fellows. Blended learning can integrate informal learning methods; it can also act as a bridge to true informal learning; well beyond the scope of the formalised training course, in that area of our lives where real work gets done. The partnership of blended and informal learning has to have a name, and so I'm going to call it Blended Learning 2.0. Groans all round, I know, but it has to be done.

This revised collection of recipes reflects the shift to a second generation of blended solutions, solutions that go well beyond the stereotypical combinations of classroom courses and self-study e-learning. Training methods are relatively timeless, but are beginning to be questioned as never before, so you'll find recipes here that demonstrate radically new approaches to learning at work. At the same time, in the three years since the first edition of this book, options for learning media have continued to multiply and evolve, providing ever more cost-effective choices for anyone responsible for assembling the blend. It seems impossible to believe that so much change will occur in the next three years, but somehow you have to believe it will.

Section one
Blended learning
is the thing

Blended learning is still the thing

Three years on from the first edition of this book and blended learning is still the thing, not so much training's big talking point any more, but certainly the strategy that most organisations are now putting into practice. Like sensitivity training, action learning, interactive video, accelerated learning, coaching and mentoring, and e-learning before it, blended learning was, at first, a bit of a bandwagon. As a result, once it had attracted widespread interest, no self-respecting member of the training cognoscenti treated it with anything other than scorn and cynicism; just another panacea to delude the masses, to fade into the background like its predecessors when we eventually realise it doesn't work. I once went to a seminar where the chairperson referred to it as the 'b' word, something not to be mentioned in polite company. I am not so shy about the subject – blended learning (there, I said it) is more than just a fad, it's a recognition that no single approach to training is versatile enough to work for all audiences, all of the time. Sometimes, only a combination of methods and media will do the job. This bandwagon may have passed through town, but it's left behind a whole load of fans who are now gearing up to provide high-quality service over the long term.

Handling objections

One of the most common objections to the razzmatazz about blended learning is that it's nothing new – blending is something we have always done. There is obviously some truth in this, because we can probably all think of some examples of training interventions that have successfully combined a variety of methods and media. But to maintain that this has been in any way the norm is clearly wide of the mark. Most learning, of course, is informal – we probably aren't even aware that it is happening.

blended learning is more than just a fad

When it is structured and formalised, it's most likely to be wholly on-job, if not wholly in the classroom, if not wholly some form of self-study. Blending has been (and still is) very much the exception, not the rule. That's not surprising because blending is a hassle; it takes more planning and more co-ordination.

Cynics may also claim that blended learning is just a rebranding exercise, carried out by e-learning vendors who hit upon hard times after the bursting of the dotcom bubble. Again, there is something to be said for this view. Most companies who claim to be in the blended learning business used to be – you guessed it – e-learning companies,

when you hear the word 'blended', run

not classroom trainers. They even tried to make the term 'blended learning' their own, referring to it as a mix of 'e-learning and traditional methods'. This definition still dominates, even though it is unhelpfully restrictive, not to say condescending about the so-called 'traditional' methods.

The e-learning community may retaliate by claiming that blended learning is in fact a sop to the classroom community, allowing them a piece of the action in a world of learning that will be increasingly dominated by the computer. This view is hard to justify. Computers are playing an increasing role in learning, but have major limitations, as we shall see. Even the most optimistic forecasts for e-learning don't see it overtaking the classroom as an approach to training.

Others object to blended learning not for what it means in theory but for how it is often applied in practice, i.e. use the classroom for anything that involves people, and then computers for the boring stuff. In his book Lessons in Learning, e-Learning and Training, Roger Schank laments that "the part that is assigned to e-learning is the rote learning part – the facts followed by the answers. That stuff doesn't stick, and for the most part trainees hate it. When you hear the word 'blended', run." Now Roger may be right – he often is – but for me what he says is really an argument for blending more effectively; being a brighter blender. Very much the point of this book.

Coming to terms with blended learning

A few years ago, I thought I had a pretty good understanding of what blended learning was about – you know, combining online and traditional elements to build courses that used the best of the old and the new. That is, until I sat at breakfast watching my wife open her Open University package; then I realised that not only was I unduly restrictive in my definition of what blended learning meant, but that when it came to imaginative combinations of ingredients, I was a complete amateur. Out of the box came workbooks, good old-fashioned text books, cassettes containing interviews, lectures and extracts from pieces of music, and books full of nothing but full-colour pictures. Then there were the TV programmes that were aired in the middle of the night for you to record and watch later, phone tutorials with your personal tutor, occasional group sessions with local members of your course and, to top it all, the one-week summer school. In this instance there wasn't a single online element (although subsequently, discussion forums and some CD-ROM based materials were added), but I defy anyone to say that this wasn't a first class example of blended learning: a broad range of media was used to present information, there were numerous self-study activities, opportunities to seek expert advice and a chance to collaborate with fellow learners (in the case of the latter, probably not enough to satisfy most learners, but a reasonable attempt given the budget). Well done the OU.

In coming to terms with blended learning, it's helpful to start with what it is not. First of all, it is not providing learners with choices of different ways to undergo a piece of training – you can have e-learning or, if you prefer, the classroom. Not only are learners failing to get a blended solution (which means they get all the disadvantages of a single approach, as well as the advantages, whereas a blend can smooth out the

> a successful blended solution is like a balanced meal, combining a range of ingredients, each of which has a unique purpose

rough edges), but you're having to pay to implement two solutions instead of one. Choice is not a bad thing, but it's likely to be a by-product of a blended solution, not the purpose.

A blended solution is also not a way of combining a number of very similar elements, say books, videos and CD-ROMs. The learner gets some variety in their self-study, but self-study is as far as it goes. A successful blended solution is like a balanced meal, combining a range of ingredients, each of which has a unique purpose.

My new, refined 2008 definition is as follows:

> "A blended learning solution combines educational and training methods within different social contexts for learning (self-study, one-to-one, group), with the aim of increasing learning effectiveness. It may also mix the learning media used to deliver the solution (face-to-face, online, offline, etc.) as a way to optimise the efficiency of the solution. These choices are made in response to particular learning requirements and audience characteristics, as well as practical constraints and opportunities."

As we shall see, research has repeatedly shown that educational and training methods have a much greater impact on the effectiveness of a learning intervention than the media which are employed to implement these methods. Assuming the media you choose do not place undue constraints on the effectiveness of the methods in question, the determining factor in selecting media is efficiency, in other words finding the medium which will consume the fewest resources and therefore be the most practical in the circumstances.

An intervention can be regarded as blended if it mixes social contexts, but not if it simply consists of a range of methods within a single context – say a number of self-study methods or a range of group activities. This distinction is necessary, otherwise practically all interventions could be classified as blended and we would be no further forward.

Although in many cases a mix of media will work best, it is also conceivable that a single broad media category (online, face-to-face, etc.) would be appropriate to support every one of the methods included in a blend. In other words, it is quite possible that an effective blend could be implemented entirely online or entirely face-to-face.

It's vital that the designer places adequate emphasis on both effectiveness and efficiency. It's easy to create blends that are effective, if you throw enough resources at the job. Similarly, it's easy to be efficient and conserve resources, if you let quality go down the pan. The challenge for the designer is to create solutions that are both effective and practical, given the inevitable resource limitations that we all work under. This should not be achieved by compromising learning effectiveness in order to save time or money; if the intervention is not effective it is not worth doing. Rather the aim is to maintain high standards of effectiveness while consuming the minimum resources, whether that's your organisation's, your learners' or your own.

Blended learning takes account of differences in learning objectives, the characteristics and preferences of learners and the practicalities of the particular situation. If you're not sensitive to these differences, the chances are you'll come up with the same familiar solution all the time, one with which you are comfortable, but not one that necessarily delivers for learners. A good example is the classic 'classroom sandwich', in which a classroom course is topped and tailed with a little e-learning. This may be the right approach in some situations; in others it could just be going through the motions.

Creating the right blends is a tough task for the twenty-first century trainer, because as soon as we started networking computers together we created a whole range of new options for delivery (online self-study, virtual classrooms, discussion forums, chat rooms and email support, not to mention podcasts and other mobile solutions), each of which has to be considered alongside more than a dozen existing options. The new

the challenge for the designer is to create solutions that are effective and practical

media have to be considered because they may prove to be more effective or more efficient for your particular mix of learning objectives, target audiences and resource constraints. What we don't need are unnecessary complications like having to include something online in the mix when it isn't needed, or having to include a non-online option when we're getting all we need from our various online options. Not to mention the fact that we don't need a blend at all for the vast majority of short courses. Now, there's a thought.

What makes good learning?

To conclude this, merely the first step in our quest for better blends for better learning, I thought it would be useful to establish some measures of success. What exactly is good learning? Would we know it if we saw it? Now we all have our own ideas on this one, but mine are the ones that count here, because these are my fingers on the keyboard.

Effective learning, at least as far as adults are concerned and in the context of their work, more than anything else needs to be relevant. When it's relevant, it matters; it makes a difference to their job performance or to their job prospects. Most open learning materials, made freely available over an organisation's intranet or in an open learning centre, are insufficiently relevant, which is why they are rarely used. Relevance is important, because if you get this right, your learner is likely to be engaged, without the need for a lot of fancy extras.

Relevance can be increased by the way that you design a learning intervention: build on the learner's existing knowledge, use plenty of examples that relate directly to the learner's work experience, make frequent use of stories and anecdotes. All of these

adult learners like to be in control

techniques are inductive in nature – they move from the specific to the general, from the concrete to the theoretical. Learners like this, because by and large they struggle to find theory relevant.

Adult learners also like to be in control. They like to determine when learning takes place (ideally just before it's needed), where it takes place and how long it lasts. Sometimes small chunks are best, sometimes sustained immersion. Sometimes they like to whip through at speed, sometimes to labour over each point. Being in control also includes the ability to ask questions whenever you want, whether that's of tutors or fellow learners; which is why pure self-study can sometimes be a let down – it denies the learner the fundamental right of questioning.

Finally, when they're at work, adults are more interested in 'knowing how' than 'knowing that'. They want skills that they can employ to their advantage in their jobs, and there's only one way to develop skills. "How do you get to Carnegie Hall?" asked the tourist in New York. "Practise," came the quick-witted response. Most training falls down because it fails to provide adequate opportunities for practice. It spends two days teaching you how to handle customer complaints, then allows you maybe ten minutes to try this out with a colleague. Just long enough, in fact, for you to realise that you can't do it. Trainers could learn from tennis coaches. They spend a few minutes demonstrating the correct strokes, then reinforce these over thousands of hours of repetitive practice.

As we shall see in subsequent chapters, almost any training approach can contribute something useful in terms of learning effectiveness; equally, every approach has inherent weaknesses which are capable of getting in the way. Often, the only way of satisfying every criterion for 'good learning' is to use a bit of this and a bit of that, which is of course where we came in.

Section two
Testing the case for
blended learning

Testing the case for blended learning

In section one, I described what I thought blended learning was all about and attempted to handle some of the more common objections raised by its detractors. I also diverted a little off the path to explore what 'good learning' might actually look like, because only when this is clear in our minds can we judge whether blending learning methods actually help us to achieve this goal.

In section two, I attempt an analysis of three broad-brush approaches – the classroom, the computer and on-job instruction – which, ironically, are not only common ingredients in a blended solution, they also represent blended learning's main competitors, when they are employed on a stand-alone basis. As a result, I hope to prove that, however strong these competitors may seem when used for the right purpose, with the right audience and at the right time, each has fatal flaws which renders them ineffective or inefficient as universal solutions. The longer, the more ambitious or the more complex a training programme becomes, the stronger the argument for adopting a blended approach. Let's see.

Why classrooms aren't enough

Even with the slow but determined growth of e-learning, the overwhelming majority of all formal, off-job training that is carried out in the workplace takes place in classrooms; this after most students have experienced 10 to 20 years of almost entirely classroom-based education. Unless teachers and trainers are all fools, which is unlikely, there must be some pretty good reasons why the classroom is so dominant. Here's a few. First and foremost, the classroom is convenient – it gathers learners together away from distractions (which in the case of adults means their jobs, but for children means opportunities for annoying adults and generally being naughty), under the guidance of a single minder, also known as a teacher, trainer or whatever. Because of the fiddle involved in gathering learners in one place (school runs, train journeys, flights, etc.), classroom sessions are traditionally measured in days rather than hours. The block-booking of learning time helps both parents/managers and learners to plan ahead. It also makes for easy administration for those people who have to book people on courses and track their progress.

The collective nature of classroom learning has other advantages. Purely economically, the bigger the class, the greater the efficiencies over one-to-one learning, albeit at the expense of individual attention. More importantly – and assuming the event

where computer networks can help, is in allowing you to share your work with tutors and colleagues, wherever they are in the world

doesn't become overly competitive – learners like being with each other. They value the potential for friendship, support and shared experience. The show-offs gain an audience. The meek can sit at the back and avoid eye contact with the trainer.

The strengths of classroom education – learning in groups, away from the work environment, at pre-determined times and for fixed periods – are, of course, also the weaknesses. The problem with groups is that they are actually a collection of individuals, with different work priorities, different starting points in terms of knowledge, skills and attitudes, and different preferences when it comes to how they learn. It is impossible to design a classroom session which, in the amount of time likely to be available, fully satisfies the needs of every participant. This difficulty is most apparent when the objective is to impart knowledge – while one person is struggling to keep up, another is twiddling their thumbs; while one is captivated by a subject that is highly relevant to their work, another is eagerly awaiting a change of topic. This is frustrating for participants; it's also highly inefficient, which is why self-study methods are typically 50 percent faster.

When the objectives become more ambitious than simply imparting knowledge, groups have more to offer. Debate and discussion can help develop understanding and influence attitudes; case studies and other group exercises can foster cognitive skills; role-plays provide an opportunity to practise interpersonal skills. While this interaction can be accomplished online, it is unlikely to be so easy to administer or facilitate. Having said this, it is important to recognise that activities carried out in the classroom are not the real thing. Working with a group on a marketing case study is not the same thing as working alone, late into the night on a real marketing campaign. Role-playing a sales call takes you only so far in preparing you to face a real customer. And many skills simply cannot be simulated in the classroom, because of the physical limitations of the space.

The other difficulty with the classroom is the necessity to gather with like-minded learners at the same place and at the same time, for a scheduled event. This requires you to travel to the event, perhaps even to stay overnight. It requires you to wait until the event is next scheduled to run, even though your needs may be urgent. It also requires you to do all your learning in a single block, when this may be more effectively – and sometimes more conveniently – handled in small chunks. And, perhaps most importantly of all, it requires you to make all the running in transferring what you have learned to the work environment. It treats learning as an event, an episode, rather than as a natural element of all working life. Events, whether they are classroom courses, concerts, plays, TV programmes or football matches, can change people's lives. More typically they are appreciated at the time, and then all too quickly forgotten.

Why computers aren't enough

When any trainer is first introduced to the concept of e-learning, they are likely to come up with the same key questions. What exactly is e-learning, and when should I use it? The first question is harder to answer than it sounds, because you have to explain all the ways that computer networks can facilitate learning, by providing learners with access to materials, to tutors and other learners. The answer to the first question then makes the second that much harder. Each form of e-learning has its own unique features and benefits, and hence its own place in the design of online and blended solutions. Nevertheless, if the trainer sticks with it, they will get to see how e-learning in its various forms can make a contribution, particularly in the teaching of knowledge – of facts, concepts, rules, principles, processes and procedures. When it comes to skills, they don't get it.

Skills are important in training because very few of us get paid for what we know; we are employed because of what we can do. It's not enough to know 'that', we have to know 'how'. If the emphasis in education is 80:20 in favour of knowing 'that', in training the priorities are reversed. So, good question, can computers really help us to learn skills? The answer, of course, is that it all depends.

Skills are rarely taught in isolation. There's typically a sequence starting with (1) the imparting of some basic supporting information, followed by (2) some sort of demonstration of the skill, then (3) the practice of that skill by the learner (ideally in a safe environment and with objective feedback), all culminating in (4) the application of the skill in the real work environment. I don't think anyone would argue that computers can help in the first step, but then that's again just a question of providing knowledge. They certainly could assist in the second, because almost any skill can be demonstrated using graphics, animation, audio or video, which, thanks to broadband,

we blend because we want our learners to achieve the best results

are all now readily available to us online. Computers might also be able to help at stage three, in providing practice with feedback, but here it depends on the type of skill.

Some skills are essentially cognitive, involving problem-solving, planning and decision-making; and in a knowledge society, a great deal of what we do falls under this category – programming, writing reports, analysing data, planning projects, creating marketing strategies. These jobs are usually carried out on a computer, so it's not too far-fetched to believe that you could practise them in the same way. The issue, of course, is how you get feedback on your code, your reports, your analyses, project plans and strategies. Computer software could be devised to examine your work and give you personalised feedback, but this is likely to be complicated and unreliable. Where computer networks can help, is in allowing you to share your work electronically with tutors and colleagues, wherever they are in the world, and to discuss your work using email, instant messaging and discussion forums.

Let's move on to interpersonal skills, the ones that involve you interacting with customers, suppliers, bosses, peers and subordinates. A fair amount of success can be achieved by designing software that helps you to take your first steps in applying these skills – scenarios that you observe and critique, scenarios in which you are an active participant and determine what happens next. However, these are first steps and not as authentic as the experiences that can be laid on in the classroom, where you have the opportunity to role-play and receive direct feedback from real humans. But even this is not enough. No skills can be learned from one or two practice sessions – the learner needs to continue their development on-the-job, getting feedback on an ongoing basis from their manager or coach.

The third category of skill is the psychomotor: practical skills that involve you interacting with the physical environment – operating machines, driving tanks, lifting parcels or cutting down trees. Classrooms and computers are of little use when it comes to practising many psychomotor skills, although there are exceptions. When the skill is computer-related, such as typing or using a mouse, then it's not surprising to find users learning on the computer itself. More important is the use of simulators to teach those skills which are too costly and too hazardous to learn in the real-world – like flying planes, operating nuclear power plants, or navigating an oil rig.

So, can computers teach skills? Well, as we've seen, they can help in the early stages of learning any skill. When the skills are cognitive, they may be able to do the whole job – less so with interpersonal and psychomotor skills. So, e-learning is no more a panacea than the classroom, which leaves us with good old Nellie.

Why Nellie's not enough

'Sitting next to Nellie', more properly known as on-job instruction, is familiar to us all, as the way we get to learn the details of our jobs when more formal approaches are not available, i.e. much of the time. Nellie's been hard at work as a part-time trainer for thousands of years, long before classrooms, books, videos and computers appeared to provide her with some much needed help. Nellie's also capable of being highly effective, providing highly individualised instruction at the point of need, whenever and wherever that may be. Nellie's pupils don't get bored because she concentrates on only the most relevant and practical issues, ignores useless theory, and places the priority on 'you doing' rather than 'her telling'. (This Nellie is, of course, idealised. Some

Nellies have been known to be unavailable, unprepared, unresponsive, impatient, rambling and even asleep. Nellies cannot be relied upon totally.)

Personal tuition is nice while it lasts, which usually means as long as you can afford it. Which is why super-rich, top-ten tennis players employ world-class coaches to travel with them on the tour, practise with them every day and generally agonise about ways of achieving one percent improvements in performance; it's also why our kids have their tennis lessons in large groups of mixed ability, get to hit only a few balls a week and more often than not remain in a state of conscious incompetence.

One-to-one tuition is intensive because you, the learner, are always working. All too often, it provides inadequate opportunities for debate, for exploration and for reflection. It rarely comes with top-quality learning materials – videos, trouble-shooting guides, white papers and checklists – which stimulate thought and provide ongoing reference. These opportunities are more likely to be provided in formal, off-job learning situations, employing – you guessed it – classrooms and computers. The fact is we need all these approaches and more; we simply cannot rely on any one of these to do the whole job in every situation. We blend because we want our learners to achieve the best results possible at every point in their training programme, within a realistic timeframe and at a realistic cost. And that's the challenge.

Section three
A logical approach
to blended learning

A logical approach to blended learning

In this third and final introductory section, I explore what I believe to be the three most important elements in a systematic approach to the design of effective and efficient blended learning solutions: analysing the unique characteristics of the situation in which the solution is to be deployed; selecting an appropriate training strategy and methods to meet the needs of the situation; and determining the communication media best suited to the chosen strategy. If this sounds abstract and theoretical, stick with me, because the process can be quickly and easily applied in practice.

First take a look at the situation

Chances are that just about every systematic approach to training that you've ever encountered starts with some form of analysis – you know, job analysis, task analysis, needs analysis, that sort of thing. You're sure that some poor trainer out there is actually doing this sort of thing, you're just glad it isn't you. Well, there's some analysis in this model as well and, sorry, it has to be conducted first, before you get onto the more enjoyable, creative bits. The reason why analysis is necessary in the real world, not only in textbooks, is because just about every training situation is different, different enough to demand a different solution. If you treat every situation the same, then you apply the same solution again and again, whether or not it is really suitable. Lazy thinking like this is what leads to catalogues full of training courses all using the same approach, such as the classroom. I know this isn't true where you work, but believe me, it happens.

One way in which situations differ is in the nature of the learning that you would like to see happen. We don't need to get into a detailed discussion here of the ways in which learning objectives can be classified, but it's important to understand what a difference these make. If your objectives have a knowledge and understanding component (a need to learn facts, principles, concepts, rules, processes, procedures, etc.), then this will influence your choice of method (because some methods are more successful than others at meeting knowledge and understanding objectives) and your subsequent choice of medium (because some of these are better suited than others to making the methods work). The same is true with other types of learning objectives (cognitive skills, interpersonal skills, psychomotor skills, attitudes) – each demands a radically different strategy, which in turn dictates the most appropriate communication medium. How different is different? Well, consider an outward bound leadership course

the process can be quickly and easily applied in practice

in the Lake District, an online, networked, marketing business game, a simulator for a military jet, an induction booklet, a negotiation skills workshop. Chances are they are trying to meet some very different objectives, wouldn't you think?

Equally important is the way in which audiences differ from one training situation to another. Of course there are the demographics – age, gender and the suchlike, which might influence your design. Of more significance is likely to be what they already know about the subject in question, what their attitude is to the subject, and what associated skills they currently possess. It matters most when these starting positions vary a great deal from person to person, because this can make it more difficult to work with them in groups (such as in a classroom) and to follow any form of uniform and fixed curriculum. The same problems can be experienced when learners differ substantially in terms of their own objectives (irrespective of what they already know or can do), because of different priorities in their jobs and careers.

Learners also differ in what psychologists like to call their 'metacognitive skills', their ability to self-direct their own learning. Some learners are more dependent than others on structure in the learning process; some are quite capable of tackling just about any subject on their own. This matters a great deal, because you simply cannot expect those with poor metacognitive skills to flourish in a free-form, exploratory learning environment. Similarly, independent learners can become frustrated by what they see as the stifling formality and rigid structure imposed by many classroom events and interactive e-learning courses.

Learners may also differ to some extent in the way they prefer to learn, whether you believe these are relatively fixed characteristics, or that they vary depending on what the learner is being asked to learn. There are various ways of modelling these differences, each with their own tests and instruments to help learners diagnose their particular preferences. What's clear, though, is that learners are quite capable of learning in any number of ways, whether or not they prefer the approach that's been selected for them. It's also clear that, unless you're sure that the majority of your audience have roughly the same preferences (it doesn't take a genius to know that you'll need to design a different course for accountants than for salespeople), there's not a lot you can do about it except to build as much variety into your course as you can; an argument for blending, perhaps?

There is one more way in which situations vary and this is in terms of the simple practicalities. Practicalities are important because training solutions have to be efficient as well as effective – working within available timescales and budgets. A number of factors influence timescales and budgets, including the geographical location of learners (because travel and subsistence are often the largest costs you'll have), the availability of facilities and equipment (because if you don't have them you'll have to buy or rent them), and the skills at your disposal in-house (because if you don't have the project managers, the designers, the trainers, the tutors and others that you need, you'll have to resource these externally, which takes time and costs more than working with what you've got).

Then you develop your strategy

Once you have a firm grasp of the situation – the type of learning required, the nature of your target audience and the practical constraints – you can begin to design an appropriate solution, starting with an appropriate overall strategy. Clark and Wittrock (2001) have a useful model for analysing strategies according to the degree of control imposed over the process by the trainer and/or the student. At the most trainer-centred end of the spectrum is simple exposition – the trainer tells the learner things, using methods such as lectures and prescribed reading; no interaction is expected or required, except perhaps some Q&A or an assessment.

The second strategy – structured instruction – is still under the trainer's overall control, but is much more interactive, allowing the trainer to fine-tune the process to the needs of the particular audience. Structured instruction is widely used in training, and includes most classroom sessions, most computer-based self-study materials and much formal on-job instruction. Dependent learners rely on this degree of structure; independent learners (which include many of those who have passed through higher education, as well as those used to taking advantage of the wider availability of knowledge through the Internet) can do without.

A more learner-centred strategy is guided discovery, in which learners engage in tasks that have been specially designed to provide them with opportunities for experimentation with alternative approaches. Learners improve their skill or understanding by reflecting, with the help of facilitators, coaches or mentors, upon the outcomes of these tasks – both the successes and the failures – and, as a result, drawing general conclusions which they can apply to future tasks. Guided discovery is experiential; it allows learners to have a go and learn from their mistakes. This strategy can be deployed in face-to-face settings, whether one-to-one, outdoors (as with Outward Bound-type courses) or in the classroom; through computer-based case studies, games and simulations; or through project work.

The final strategy is exploration – each learner determines their own learning process, taking advantage of resources provided by trainers and others, and takes out of this process their own, unique learning. Exploration may seem a relatively informal strategy, but no less useful for that. In fact it's probably the way that most learning takes place.

The learning process underlying any of these top-level strategies is likely to have a number of key stages or elements, for example: preparing the learner, presenting learning content, providing opportunities for practice, offering feedback, providing

technology has increased the selection of media available to teachers and trainers

opportunities for reflection and planning, application to the real-job environment, providing ongoing support. The exact nature of these stages or elements will depend on your objectives and your chosen strategy. The important issue here is that you attempt to separate out those aspects of the learning process that are very different in character, because there is a good chance that you'll benefit from applying different methods and different media to the different elements. This is where the opportunities arise for blended learning. If you can't sensibly break down the process for your given situation, that's not a problem – you can probably save yourself some trouble and use a single medium.

Only now do you select the medium

You'll want to flesh out your strategy by selecting specific methods for use at each stage. There are hundreds to choose from, a selection of which are listed in Appendix 3. Note that very few of these methods are tied to a specific learning medium – they can usually be applied in more than one way, perhaps online, face-to-face, even over the phone. It's an important aspect of this approach to blended learning that you leave the choice of medium until last. First you establish the methods that you believe will be effective in meeting the demands of your particular session. You then select the most appropriate medium for each of these methods, looking to optimise efficiency without compromising on effectiveness. If you choose more than one medium, you have a blend. If the same medium works in each case, you do not.

Let's just pause for a moment to make absolutely clear how methods and media impact on the likely success of your solution. Broadly speaking methods determine effectiveness – if you choose the right methods, you are likely to achieve your learning objectives. Educational and training methods are relatively stable in that the range of options doesn't change much over time. Much the same possibilities – lectures, discussions, games, demonstrations, assessments, reading assignments, coaching sessions and so on – were available as readily 500 years ago as now. True, the trends in methods do change periodically in response to new research, philosophies or politics, but the toolkit stays much the same.

A great deal of effort has been put into research to test whether the communications media used for learning have a similar impact on effectiveness. Thomas L. Russell undertook an analysis of more than 350 studies conducted over the past 50 years, each attempting to compare the effectiveness of one learning medium with another. The title of Russell's book is The No Significant Difference Phenomenon, which says it all. A meta-analysis of 96 studies by Sitzmann and others in 2006, makes clear that it's the instructional method, not the delivery medium, that makes the difference. When web-based instruction and classroom instruction that employed similar methods were compared, there was little or no difference in outcomes. Where the choice of medium really matters is in the effect it has on the *efficiency* of the solution.

Technology has increased the selection of media available to teachers and trainers. Of course all learning was originally conducted face-to-face, providing an immediacy to

methods and media impact on the success of your solution

the interaction, a rich sensory experience (you see, you hear, you touch, you smell) and, if you're lucky enough to be one-on-one, the ultimate in personalisation. Books, when they arrived, provided the counterbalance, by allowing learners more independence and the ability to control the pace. The invention of the telephone provided additional connectivity for learners and tutors working at a distance. Videos, CDs and all their variants added to the diversity of offline media and made high-quality audio and video available to distance learners. But perhaps the most significant new medium made available by technology is the networked computer, connecting learners to more than a billion other Internet users and countless billions of web pages. E-learning is the rather inadequate name we give to the use of networked computers as a medium to facilitate learning. It is more a media category than a single medium, because it is capable of supporting a wide variety of different tools and techniques, many of which have almost certainly not yet been invented.

A little pragmatism

Systematic approaches are rarely followed to the letter in the real world – after all, let's face it, life's just too short. What's important is that when we cut corners, we do so consciously, applying the main principles with common sense and a great deal of pragmatism. The rest of this book is laden with examples of typical training situations and uncomplicated blended solutions. If you find it hard (or simply too boring) to apply the systematic approach, you're welcome to copy any of the examples which you find relevant to your experience. The end result should be the same – more effective, efficient training solutions.

Section four
Recipes

Recipe 1: Product updates

The situation

The organisation is a large multinational electronics company, with a catalogue of thousands of products. New products are launched practically every week, typically offering minor variants and improvements on existing products.

The organisation needs to keep its international sales force and team of engineers conversant with the new products. This requires that they know the major discriminating characteristics of each new product, the benefits that these afford the customer, and the implications these have for technical support and maintenance.

The audience for the training consists of technically competent and experienced professionals, who already have a good understanding of the organisation's product line. They are widely distributed geographically, working from country offices or from their homes, but have easy broadband access to the organisation's intranet. Their busy schedule of appointments allows them only a minimal time to spend on product training.

The training for each new product must be prepared and delivered prior to launch, a lead time of a couple of weeks at best. With their other responsibilities, product managers and technical trainers have little time to devote to new product training.

The strategy

The organisation has chosen to use an exposition strategy. They believe that the target audience are sufficiently independent learners and have sufficient experience to benefit from this approach. It also allows them to prepare and deliver the training in a minimum of time.

The blend

Elements	Methods	Media
Preparation	Announce the training	Email / SMS messaging
Delivery	Presentation of the product	Virtual classroom
	Q&A	Virtual classroom
	Viewing recorded video material	Recording of virtual classroom session (for those that miss the live session)
Application	Performance support / reference	Web pages on intranet
		Downloadable PDF documents

The rationale

The organisation has chosen to use online media exclusively to fulfil this strategy, an obvious choice given the wide geographic distribution of the audience, time constraints and ready availability of technology. The primary delivery mechanism is a virtual classroom, providing the ability for the trainer to speak to the audience live with audio, to show slides and handle any questions. The session could be run more than once to accommodate different time zones.

The performance support materials provide easy ongoing reference at a much greater level of detail, making use of existing marketing and technical reference materials.

Recipe 2: Detailed policies and procedures

The situation

The organisation is the credit card division of a major bank. The bank is re-organising its call centres so that all operators will be capable of handling all types of calls, whereas in the past, different departments had specialised in particular aspects of the customer relationship (new accounts, customer service, credit and collection, etc.).

The learning consists almost entirely of rules and procedures. The sum total of these is considerable, although all learners will have had experience of a sizeable slice (perhaps 25 percent). Some of the rules and procedures apply generally across many circumstances. Others are likely to be applied only in exceptional circumstances.

Two thousand learners need to be trained. Although they have experience of the subject matter, they are not typically independent learners and will benefit from a structured approach. On the whole, they tend to enjoy practical activity and interaction with their peers.

Operators are split evenly between three major centres around the UK, each with its own classroom training facilities. The training department has four months in which to design and implement the solution, which should have the minimum possible impact on the ongoing business. The department has plenty of skilled and qualified trainers for whom this training is their main priority. They also have funds to engage outside suppliers if necessary.

The strategy

The organisation has chosen to use a structured instruction strategy, based on the nature of the learning required and the characteristics of the target audience. The group sessions also incorporate an element of guided discovery using case studies, scenarios and group discussion.

The blend

Elements	Methods	Media
Preparation	Reading (about the training and how it will be organised)	Web pages on intranet
Delivery (to address only the most general rules and procedures)	Group instruction	Classroom
	Group activities / exercises (case studies and scenarios)	Classroom
	Facilitated group discussion	Classroom
	Group progress review	Classroom

The rationale

The most important feature of this approach is the decision to restrict the formal delivery element to the most general rules and procedures. This shortens the training considerably and avoids the danger of overload. It also makes time available for the more important rules to be properly explored and discussed. The classroom was chosen because of the availability of trainers and classroom facilities, the fact that learners would not have to travel to the sessions, the fact that training could be accomplished in a single session, and the suitability of the setting for group work and discussion.

The intranet was chosen for the reference material because of its availability to every learner at their desktop, the speed with which information could be accessed and the ease with which material could be maintained.

Recipe 3: In-company MBA course

The situation

The organisation is a large multinational company with regional headquarters in Brussels, Singapore and Dallas. They are organising an in-house, two-year Master of Business Administration course for 24 middle-managers, split evenly across the three regional offices.

The learning will be academic in nature, made more relevant, where possible, by practical work centring on issues faced by individual participants and the company as a whole. Expected learning outcomes include a broad knowledge and understanding of business issues, as well as advanced problem-solving skills.

Learners are aged between 28 and 45, mostly graduates, with several years' management experience and an ability to learn independently where required. All are fluent in English as a first or second language.

The distance between the regional centres is a major practical constraint.

The strategy

The faculty has decided to adopt a mixed approach of simple exposition, for delivery of the core curriculum, guided discovery as a way of building understanding and problem-solving skills, with an element of exploration in the work towards the assignments.

The blend

Elements	Methods	Media
Preparation	Reading (about the course)	Web pages within the Virtual Learning Environment (VLE)
	Individual questionnaire (to assess prior knowledge, personal goals, learning preferences, potential problems, etc.)	Online (accessed from the VLE)
	Syndicate group presentation and facilitated discussion	Face-to-face small group meeting (tutor travels to the home country of the syndicate group)
	Ice-breaking activity (whole group)	Discussion forum (part of VLE)
	One-to-one coaching / support	Email Telephone
Delivery of core curriculum (interspersed with practical work below)	Lectures	Virtual classroom
	Prescribed reading	Books
	One-to-one subject matter support	Email Telephone
Practical work	Syndicate group activities (case studies, scenarios)	Participants communicate locally face-to-face, by email and telephone; results are shared using the forum
	Inter-syndicate group business game	Game is run online; communication as above
	Syndicate group assignments	Communication as above
	Unfacilitated syndicate group discussion (for planning / reflection)	Face-to-face (locally)
	Facilitated group discussion	Discussion forum

Elements	Methods	Media
Assessment	Individual project / assignment	N/A
	One-to-one progress review	Email Telephone
Review	Group progress review	Discussion forum

The rationale

Because of the distance problem, the organisation has opted for online communication within the group as a whole as well as for lectures (using a virtual classroom). Care will have to be taken in scheduling these live events to take consideration of time zone differences, although they can be recorded for those not able to attend at the scheduled time. The majority of communication is asynchronous, using discussion forums, email and web documents.

Syndicate groups are able to work together locally, including face-to-face sessions where required. Note how the tutor travels to meet with the syndicate groups at the start of the programme.

Recipe 4: Telephone customer service

The situation

The organisation is a government department that is soon to launch a new help line for businesses. To provide this service they have employed 200 new staff to work in a brand-new call centre. They have already provided the staff with an induction to the organisation and training is in progress to familiarise staff with the information they will be expected to supply to callers. To ensure a consistently high level of customer service, the organisation now requires all staff to receive telephone customer service training.

The primary learning objective is to develop interpersonal skills, although there is an attitudinal component as well.

The audience varies in the amount of telephone customer service experience they possess. The majority are not used to learning independently.

There are few practical constraints as all staff are working in the same centre, which has excellent training facilities, including computer classrooms. However, a shortage of time means that not everyone will be able to receive group training before the help line opens.

The strategy

The training department has decided to adopt a structured instruction strategy, believing that the audience will respond better to a structured approach and that the strategy is well suited to the training of interpersonal skills.

The blend

Elements	Methods	Media
Preparation	Group presentations (to provide an overview of the training programme and handle queries)	Classroom

Elements	Methods	Media
Preliminary training	Interactive self-study lessons	Online over the intranet (using customised off-the-shelf materials)
	Individual activities and exercises (including case studies and scenarios)	Online over the intranet (using customised off-the-shelf materials)
	One-to-one progress review	Face-to-face
Primary skills training	Group ice-breaking activity	Classroom
	Group instruction	Classroom
	Facilitated group discussion	Classroom
	Individual practice (observed by the trainer and the learners)	Classroom
	Group progress review	Classroom
Ongoing skill development	One-to-one coaching	Face-to-face

The rationale

An important decision has been made to provide preliminary training on a self-study basis (although they could also allow this training to take place at the computer in twos or threes). This solves two problems: first, the variability in learners' customer service experience; and second, the need for some foundation knowledge and skills to be imparted before learners get the opportunity to attend the classroom sessions. The face-to-face progress reviews ensure learners are able to resolve any difficulties they are experiencing with the self-study materials.

The classroom has been selected for the primary skills training, as this provides a better environment for skills practice using role play exercises, and discussion of customer service issues. Because all learners will have completed the preliminary training, all members of the classroom group will have the same foundation knowledge and skills.

Because continued practice and feedback is essential, ongoing coaching is provided face-to-face in the workplace.

Recipe 5: Retail induction

The situation

The organisation is a fast-growing UK retail fashion chain appealing primarily to a young audience and with a reputation for 'attitude'. The company's offices and warehouses are based at one location in the Midlands. They are looking to set up a new company induction programme to be taken by all new full-time staff before they join their branches or departments.

The company wants to use the company induction to familiarise new starters with the company's history, culture and business values. It would also like new starters to be aware of the basic mechanics of the business and the critical factors driving its success in a highly-competitive market. More detailed training in company policies will follow.

The majority of new starters are outgoing young people with an interest in fashion and a modern lifestyle. They are likely to be tech-savvy. Many of them will have had no previous retail experience, other than perhaps the odd part-time job. Only a minority will have gone through higher education.

Between 10 and 20 new starters join the company every week, primarily to work in branches around the UK. The company would like the company induction to be brief but high impact.

The strategy

The company has decided to divide the induction into three phases: self-study work carried out by learners individually before joining, a formal induction session on day one, and a resource for ongoing reference. To make the self-study as interesting and challenging as possible, they have adopted a guided discovery strategy, using games and quizzes to stimulate learners to find out information about the company from the textual, graphical and video resources provided.

The session on day one utilises a simple exposition strategy, with the aim of filling in any gaps in knowledge and understanding left by the pre-work. Key messages are reinforced in the process of visits to the various head office departments and the warehouse.

The blend

Elements	Methods	Media
Before joining the company	Games (used as a catalyst for learners to search out information about the company)	Online (Internet)
	Recorded video material	Online (Internet)
	Reading	Web pages (Internet)
On day one	Group presentation (welcome, overview of the day, etc.)	Classroom
	Group visits to key departments in the office and to the warehouse	In work environment, accompanied by trainer
	Group subject-matter support (Q&A)	Classroom
Ongoing support	Performance support / reference	Web pages (intranet)

The rationale

The Internet is used for the pre-work, on the assumption that employees have access to PCs and an Internet connection. In exceptional cases, the material could be provided on CD-ROM. Having this material online allows for easy updating.

Face-to-face methods are utilised for day one, allowing new starters to receive a personal welcome, socialise with each other, look around head office and gain immediate answers to their questions.

The intranet is used for ongoing support so that material can be easily accessed at any time and can be readily updated.

Recipe 6: Selling skills for financial advisers

The situation

The organisation is a large insurance company with a network of several thousand financial advisers, working from small offices and their own homes. The company is aware that sales opportunities are being lost because many of the advisers are not employing best practice selling skills and wishes to bridge this gap using a training resource.

The primary learning requirement is for interpersonal skills, although some underpinning knowledge is also required.

The financial advisers come from a variety of backgrounds and have differing levels of selling skills. As mature adults, they are relatively independent learners, strongly motivated to improve their results and thereby gain higher commissions. They are essentially pragmatists, looking for any ideas that they can apply straight away.

Because of an increased priority being placed on compliance training to meet FSA requirements, the company is reluctant to take salespeople off-job for sales skills training as well. This view is endorsed by the financial advisers for whom days away mean lost sales opportunities.

All of the advisers are issued with laptops and PDAs (Personal Digital Assistants – palmtop computers). Their managers are able to join them in the field from time to time, but have too many commitments to do this regularly.

The strategy

The company has decided to adopt two strategies employing the same learning materials. For those advisers requiring a more formal introduction to selling skills, they will use structured instruction. As an ongoing resource for all advisers, they will use an exploration strategy, allowing advisers to make use of the materials as they see fit.

The blend

Elements	Methods	Media
Formal sales training	Interactive self-study materials (to cover the underpinning knowledge)	Online over the intranet (with option to download for offline use on PDAs)
	Recorded video material (to demonstrate sales skills in a wide variety of situations)	As above
	One-to-one subject matter support ('ask the expert')	Email
	Facilitated group discussion	Discussion forum
	One-to-one coaching	Face-to-face (with managers)
Ongoing performance support	As above, but accessed on an on-demand, just-in-time basis	As above

The rationale

The learning materials are organised as a library of learning objects which can be fashioned into formal courses or accessed on a random-access basis via an LCMS (Learning Content Management System). This library will be continuously updated with further video demonstrations, case histories and other resources. As all advisers have access to laptops with broadband connections, these learning objects are made available online, with the option of downloading to the PDAs for just-in-time use on the road.

The face-to-face coaching is an important ingredient, because this allows advisers to get personalised feedback based on their performance, something that would be almost impossible to achieve online.

Recipe 7: Continuous professional development

The situation

The organisation is a large professional firm employing hundreds of consultants, the majority of whom work most of the time on customer premises. The requirement is to provide continuous professional development for the consultants to ensure they are kept abreast of all the latest ideas, developments and legislation.

The consultants are highly-educated and technically-literate young professionals, with the potential to learn independently. They travel to customer premises by train, car and plane and spend many nights in hotels.

Every consultant is equipped with a laptop and an iPod.

The strategy

The firm has decided to meet the requirement using a mix of exposition and exploration strategies, which are well-suited to the dissemination of information and knowledge when learners are not required to formally demonstrate what they have learned. They are satisfied that the audience is sufficiently independent and experienced to be able to cope with these approaches without difficulty.

The blend

Elements	Methods	Media
Delivery	Recorded audio material (monologues and interviews)	Downloadable MP3 files delivered as podcasts
	Group lectures / presentations, including Q&A	'Webinars' using virtual classroom software
	Reading (in-depth coverage of the issues raised in the above)	Web pages on intranet
	Facilitated group discussion of topics raised above	Discussion forum
	Individual exploration / research	Using web links listed on intranet web pages

The rationale

The media have in this case been chosen to provide flexible access to learners on the move and working off-site. The use of podcasts makes it possible for learners to catch up on the latest information while travelling and while not online. The webinars and bulletin boards allow issues to be clarified, explored and debated in greater depth. Only the webinars are 'live' and require learners to be online at a specific time, although these could also be viewed later as recordings.

Recipe 8: Leadership training

The situation

The organisation is a major charity delivering overseas aid. Their requirement is for leadership training for their middle managers at head office and working in the field. They wish their managers to achieve a balance in their leadership behaviour between the needs of the task, the needs of the individuals in the team, and the needs of the team as a whole.

The audience consists of well-educated and motivated professionals, aged from mid-twenties to late fifties. All have leadership experience, in some cases a considerable amount.

Head office employees are based on a single site, with a fully-equipped training centre. Employees working in the field are geographically dispersed but have access to the Internet.

The strategy

The charity has decided to adopt a guided discovery strategy, because processes, principles and attitudes are essential aspects of the requirement. This strategy should also work well for learners with a reasonable amount of experience of leadership.

The blend

Elements	Methods	Media
Preparation	Questionnaire completed by student, manager, subordinates, peers (360°), to assess starting position	Online activity
Delivery	Group ice-breaking activity	Workshop
	Group activities / exercises	Workshop
	Unfacilitated group discussion (for planning and reflection)	Workshop

Elements	Methods	Media
	Facilitated whole group discussion (to draw out general conclusions)	Workshop
	Individual action planning activity	N/A
Application	Individual work experience	N/A
	Individual reflection activity	Learners each maintain a blog
	Unfacilitated group discussion	Learners comment on each others' blog entries
	One-to-one coaching	Tutors respond to learners' blog entries by adding comments
Review	Further 360° questionnaire to assess shift in perceptions / changes in behaviour	Online activity
	Group progress review	Virtual classroom
	Facilitated group discussion	Virtual classroom

The rationale

A key component of the programme is a workshop, during which learners experiment with leadership behaviour and obtain feedback through the results they achieve with the group activities and from other group members. Although it is expensive for employees working in the field to attend the workshop, the charity feels there is no feasible alternative to a face-to-face setting. Learners prepare for the workshop with a 360° feedback exercise, completed online. At the end of the workshop they make plans to apply what they have learned to the work environment.

Following the workshop, learners maintain a daily learning blog, accessible by all members of the group. The blog encourages learners to reflect on and share their real-world leadership experiences. After one month, the 360° feedback exercise is repeated and the group reconvenes online for a short review workshop.

Recipe 9: Training for air traffic controllers

The situation

The organisation is an international air traffic control training school, providing comprehensive training programmes for new air traffic controllers.

The learning requirement is multi-faceted, including knowledge of concepts, processes, principles, rules and procedures; operation of technical equipment; and advanced problem-solving and decision-making skills. Learners are typically in their twenties and thirties, computer-literate, but varying somewhat in their knowledge and experience of aviation issues.

During the period of the training, learners are residential at the training centre. Once back with their employers, they have ongoing Internet access.

The strategy

The school has chosen a strategy of structured instruction, with an element of guided discovery using simulators. It believes these strategies are the most appropriate given the emphasis on imparting knowledge and cognitive skills, and the fact that many of the learners are relative novices.

The blend

Elements	Methods	Media
Background knowledge	Interactive self-study lessons	Online over the school's intranet using their own bespoke materials, within a computer classroom
	Group activities	Classroom
	Facilitated group discussion	Classroom
	Group visit (to observe air traffic controllers at work)	N/A

Elements	Methods	Media
Skills development	Group instruction	Classroom
	Repeated individual practice (observed by trainer and other learners)	Dedicated simulators (within the school)
	Group progress reviews	Classroom
Application (on return from school)	Observed practice on live system	On-job
	Performance support / reference	Web pages on the Internet / downloadable PDFs

The rationale

The background knowledge element is largely accomplished in the classroom, using a mix of interactive self-study lessons and group work. The self-study component is helpful because it allows students to work at their own pace, which is important when there is a great deal of technical material to be covered and the level of starting knowledge varies. This is complemented by group activities and discussion, providing opportunities to integrate, expand on and reinforce the material.

Simulators are used to allow learners to experience a wide variety of potential situations without a risk to safety. When learners return from the school they continue to develop their skills on-job with an experienced controller.

The school provides materials for ongoing reference online, so they can be accessed easily by past students wherever they are based, and so the materials can be continuously maintained and improved.

Recipe 10: Developing presentation skills

The situation

The organisation is a small training company providing coaching to those wishing to develop their presentation skills. The company is headed up by an internationally-renown expert on public speaking and communication.

The programme provided by the company includes a knowledge component (essential concepts, principles and rules) but is primarily focused on building communication skills.

Typical learners are middle and senior managers, as well as sales and marketing professionals. All will have had experience of presenting and all will have the capability to learn independently if required. On the whole they are cash-rich and time-poor. They are also not keen to show up any frailties in their abilities in front of their peers.

The strategy

The company employs a mix of exposition, guided discovery and exploration, all geared towards experienced, independent learners who want highly individualised attention.

The blend

Elements	Methods	Media
Preparation	Individual questionnaire (to help learners clarify their personal objectives)	Online activity
	One-to-one planning session	Telephone
	Individual practice (the learner makes a real presentation, observed by coach)	Either face-to-face (coach attends a presentation given by the learner) or remote (the learner submits a video of a presentation for the coach to review)

Elements	Methods	Media
	Reading (materials written by the founder of the company)	Book
	Viewing recorded video material (featuring skills demonstrations)	DVD
Coaching	One-to-one coaching	Face-to-face
	Individual assignment (learner prepares a presentation outline and submits to coach for review)	Submitted and responded to using email
	Individual assignment (learner prepares slides and submits to coach for review)	Submitted and responded to using email
	Individual practice (the learner makes a real presentation, observed by coach – as above)	Either face-to-face or remote using video (as above)
	[These four steps cycle as required]	
Application	Performance support / ongoing reinforcement	Downloadable MP3 files (played from the PC or as podcasts)
		Web pages on Internet (including a regular blog by the founder)

The rationale

The programme utilises offline media (books and DVD) – easily accessible anytime and anywhere – to introduce background knowledge and demonstrate core skills. Some of the coaching is face-to-face, allowing the coach to build a strong relationship with the learner and providing opportunities for some one-to-one skills practice. At other times the dialogue continues online, primarily for the learner's convenience.

When the programme has been completed, the relationship with the learner is maintained and the key concepts reinforced by regular online communications.

Recipe 11: Training for network engineers

The situation

The organisation is an IT training company providing technical courses for IT professionals around the world. The requirement is for comprehensive training for computer engineers working on large-scale corporate networks using a wide range of hardware and software configurations.

Learners must first acquire a certain amount of background knowledge about networking (concepts, processes, principles, rules, etc.). This then needs to be applied to the technical problem-solving tasks which form the most important element of their work.

Learners are typically in their twenties and thirties, bright and technically-literate. Because they have different amounts of work experience, they vary considerably in their starting level of knowledge of the subject. Their preference is to learn through hands-on experience wherever possible.

It is prohibitively expensive to equip classrooms with the wide range of networking hardware and software required for learners to have the hands-on practice they need. On the other hand, it would be too risky for learners to practise using live networks.

The strategy

The training company has chosen to employ a mix of structured instruction and guided discovery strategies, the former for background knowledge and the latter as the basis for developing the key problem-solving skills.

The blend

Elements	Methods	Media
Background knowledge	Interactive self-study lessons	Online over the Internet
	One-to-one subject matter support	Email and instant messaging
	Individual assessment	Online over the Internet
Practical work	Individual assignments (tasks to be completed using real network hardware and software)	Online over the Internet using online labs (see description below)
	One-to-one subject matter support	Email and instant messaging
	One-to-one progress review	Email and instant messaging
Application	Performance support / reference	Web pages on the Internet
		Downloadable PDF documents

The rationale

The company has used interactive self-study to provide the background knowledge, because this allows learners to learn at their own pace, and in their own preferred time and place. This is particularly important given the wide variability in their starting knowledge.

Practical work is provided through online labs, which allow learners to configure real network hardware and software (provided at a central location by the training company) at a distance over the Internet. This provides a more realistic experience than a simulation, but avoids the risks associated with practising with a live system.

Individual work is backed up at all stages by online tutorial support, accessible by email and instant messaging.

Recipe 12: Healthy living

The situation

The organisation is the head office of a major insurance company, employing about 1,000 white-collar workers. On the initiative of the occupational health department, they have decided to conduct a programme to educate staff about the benefits of exercise and healthy eating, and to encourage them to make positive changes in their lifestyle.

A certain amount of background knowledge is required, in the form of facts, concepts, processes, rules and principles. These need to be considered in the context of learners' existing attitudes and behaviours.

The programme is voluntary, so is only likely to attract those with a degree of motivation to change. Learners will vary widely in their age, prior knowledge and learning preferences.

Given that all participants are based at the same site, there are few practical constraints, other than that the programme should be conducted outside normal office hours.

The strategy

The programme uses a certain amount of structured instruction to provide learners with the background knowledge and understanding that they require. However, to encourage lasting changes to attitudes and behaviour, the more learner-centred strategies of guided discovery and exploration are employed as the programme progresses.

The blend

Elements	Methods	Media
Preparation	Questionnaire	Paper-based
	Short presentation and Q&A	Classroom
	Group discussion (review of questionnaire results)	Classroom

Elements	Methods	Media
Delivery	Interactive self-study lessons	CD-ROM (for use at home or work)
Application	Individual assignments (diets, exercise regimes, etc.)	N/A
	Group activities (hikes, runs, etc.)	N/A
	Individual reflection activity	Learners each maintain a blog
	Unfacilitated group discussion	Learners comment on each others' blog entries
	Weekly group progress reviews and discussions	Classroom
	Ongoing reference (including links to web resources)	Web pages on intranet

The rationale

The programme includes an important face-to-face ingredient, which provides an opportunity for free discussion, and allows the group to bond and provide mutual support. The fact that these sessions take place every week is also important in keeping up peer pressure and providing encouragement.

The self-study element provides those learners who need structure with a step-by-step route to acquiring the necessary knowledge and understanding. This material would need to be engaging, highly interactive and encourage reflection. More independent learners could explore the online reference materials and web links.

The requirement for learners to complete a learning journal in the form of a blog maintains the programme's momentum between classroom sessions, encouraging openness and collaboration.

Recipe 13: Language learning

The situation

The organisation is a manufacturer of defence equipment which has recently agreed a major, long-term partnership deal with a French firm. This will involve them working closely together on a number of new development projects. To encourage a close and friendly relationship with their partner, the company is initiating a three-month-long campaign to improve the French-language skills of around 100 employees who will be assigned to the projects from the beginning.

Learners will be expected to achieve only a basic level of capability with written and spoken French, as English will be the business language and French-fluent personnel will be assigned to posts requiring close liaison.

The target audience consists primarily of engineers, well-educated but with only basic school French, working at one major site. They will be allowed a certain amount of time off each week to complete the programme, but could not be released for intensive, face-to-face courses.

The strategy

The programme employs a structured instruction strategy, which is well suited to the systematic teaching of vocabulary, grammar and communication skills.

The blend

Elements	Methods	Media
Preparation	One-to-one pre-assessment	Face-to-face
Delivery	Interactive self-study lessons (with audio and video)	CD-ROM (for use at home or work)
	Weekly, 90-minute sessions including group instruction and practical conversational exercises	Classroom

Elements	Methods	Media
	Individual written assignments	Submitted by email to tutor for assessment
	Individual and group assignments, including periods of communicating with each other only in French, whether face-to-face, by email or on the telephone	N/A

The rationale

The programme requires a face-to-face component, so learners can practise their conversational French and receive feedback. These activities could also be undertaken in a virtual classroom, but this facility is not needed because learners are all based on the same site.

The self-study component allows learners to acquire basic vocabulary and grammar at their own pace, and at a time and place that suits them. This will be individually tailored depending on learners' performance in the initial one-to-one assessments.

The programme also makes use of the real working environment to provide opportunities for ongoing practice.

Recipe 14: Diversity training

The situation

The organisation is a telecommunications company employing around 2,000 white collar and blue collar staff. As part of a broad management initiative to encourage a more diverse and harmonious workforce, and to avoid claims arising because of infringements to equal opportunities legislation, the company intends to have all employees participate in a diversity training programme. There is a small knowledge component to the training, but the main requirement is to shift attitudes positively towards diversity both as a concept and in terms of actual behaviour.

Learners vary dramatically in terms of age, educational level, the type of work they do and their existing attitudes to diversity. Most are technically literate and all have access to computers, whether at their desk, in dedicated learning centres or at home.

The strategy

The company has chosen to adopt a guided discovery approach to the training, as they feel this provides the best chance to positively influence attitudes.

The blend

Elements	Methods	Media
Preparation	Confidential questionnaire regarding attitudes to diversity (pre-course)	Online on the intranet
	One-hour interactive self-study programme, including stories, personal accounts and case studies	CD-ROM (for use at home or work)

Elements	Methods	Media
Delivery	Group ice-breaking activity	Classroom
	Group activities including games and role-plays	Classroom
	Facilitated group discussion	Classroom
Application	Reading (case studies, updates to legislation, etc.)	Web pages on intranet
	Facilitated group discussion	Discussion forum
Evaluation	Confidential questionnaire regarding attitudes to diversity (post-course)	Online on the intranet

The rationale

The centrepiece of the course is a face-to-face workshop in which learners participate in a series of activities designed to provide new perspectives on diversity. These activities need to be conducted in a social context in which learners find it easy to reflect and share their thoughts and experiences, making the classroom the obvious choice.

The introductory CD-ROM allows learners to acquire a basic knowledge of diversity concepts and current legislation in their own time. It also raises a number of issues for learners to reflect on in advance of the workshop.

The intranet provides a means to keep the messages from the course alive and to encourage ongoing debate using a discussion forum.

Recipe 15: Basic literacy

The situation

The organisation is a training provider specialising in adult numeracy and literacy. They have a contract to provide basic literacy training to employees of a major car manufacturer wishing to develop their skills in order to improve their career prospects.

The learning is essentially knowledge-based, comprising facts, concepts, rules and principles.

Typical learners are poorly educated and likely to have had unhappy past experiences of learning. They have access to computers and meeting room facilities in the company's open learning centre.

The strategy

The training provider uses structured instruction to meet the requirement, which is well suited to the nature of the subject and provides the structure that these learners are likely to require.

The blend

Elements	Methods	Media
Preparation	One-to-one review	Face-to-face
Delivery	Interactive self-study lessons	Online over the Internet
	Individual drill and practice	Online over the Internet
	Written assignments	Submitted as email attachments; feedback by email
	One-to-one coaching (one hour per fortnight)	Face-to-face

Elements	Methods	Media
Application	Ongoing reference	Web pages on the Internet
	One-to-one subject matter support	Email

The rationale

Although the coaching relationship could have been conducted entirely online, the provider has chosen to mix in a regular face-to-face element, to provide additional structure and personal support to learners who are unlikely to want to work entirely independently.

Otherwise, the key literacy concepts are delivered using interactive lessons and drill and practice exercises, accessed online. These allow learners to work at their own pace and obtain the amount of intensive practice required if they are to significantly improve their skills.

The written assignments are submitted and reviewed online, reducing the need for face-to-face contact time.

Recipe 16: Handling customer complaints

The situation

The organisation is a large multinational telecommunications company based in London. The organisation has realised that customer service is a key differentiator in its market and that if they can provide higher levels of service then this will help them to retain customers and to win new business. The organisation is also finding that the process of dealing with complaints is putting an enormous amount of stress on employees.

The learning requirement is multi-faceted: instilling the motivation to ensure that complaints are dealt with efficiently, developing the soft skills to handle customers sensitively, and providing knowledge of the processes and procedures that need to be followed.

Because of the high volume of sales that the organisation is currently managing, approximately 1,500 employees need to be trained in complaint handling.

The strategy

The organisation has chosen to use a structured instruction strategy, applied using a wide variety of learning media in a blended approach.

The blend

Elements	Methods	Media
Preparation	Collecting examples of good and bad customer service	Email / paper / anecdotes
Motivation	Viewing recorded video material (demonstrating the cost of losing a customer)	DVDs in the classroom
	Facilitated group discussion about the importance of handling complaints effectively	Classroom

Elements	Methods	Media
Soft skills	Individual practice using role play exercises	Classroom
Processes and procedures	Interactive self-study materials, providing proof of learning; these are scenario based, asking learners how they would respond to a situation and then providing feedback	Online over the intranet
	Performance support / reference	Paper-based job aids
Ongoing support	Coaching to help learners maintain their motivation and their customer handling skills	Group surgeries One-to-one support

The rationale

An important objective of this training is to maintain high levels of motivation in the workplace. The organisation felt that this would be best accomplished using video and discussion in a classroom setting.

It is important for regulatory reasons that employees follow a specific complaint handling procedure and this was trained most efficiently using a one hour e-learning module, backed up by job aids. The e-learning provides proof of learning, which is important as this training is a key element of a strategy designed to retain and win back customers.

Recipe 17: Electronic records management system

The situation

The organisation is a large government department located across multiple sites in the UK. In response to e-Government initiatives, a new Electronic Records Management System (ERM) is being installed.

About 5,000 employees need to know about the new system and its related processes and procedures, but the key to success is winning over hearts and minds and convincing staff that change is not only necessary but beneficial. The department believes there could be a great deal of resistance to the change and that they therefore need to take a 'hand holding' approach.

An important secondary objective is the department's desire to pilot e-learning.

As this is a high profile project, it requires a substantial internal marketing effort over a sustained period.

The strategy

The department has chosen to adopt a mix of learning strategies, including guided discovery in the process of building motivation, structured instruction for teaching the processes and procedures, and an element of exploration in the wide variety of follow-up methods.

The blend

Elements	Methods	Media
Motivation	Group presentations in the form of roadshows to explain the planned changes; delivered by senior civil servants six months prior to the training	Face-to-face events
	Group presentation and discussion in the form of structured meetings with their managers, designed to reinforce the roadshows and provide a channel to address concerns	Face-to-face meetings
Marketing	Reading material provided through a website available six months before the launch and providing an identity for the project	Online over the intranet
	A series of pioneering pilot projects across the department; each is high profile, given high visibility and used to positively promote the change	N/A
Processes and procedures	Workshops designed to provide a high level overview of the new system, including hands-on practical sessions	Classroom
	Scenario-based, interactive self-study materials	A Learning Zone with allocated slots for each employee. Twenty employees at a time complete a two-hour e-learning course with floorwalkers available for support

Elements	Methods	Media
Follow-up	Opportunity to refresh the self-study training	Learning Café allowing employees to drop in for a refresher of the training and ask questions in a relaxed environment
	Performance support / reference in the form of a desktop-based, step-by-step guide, providing show-me, try-me functionality	Online over the intranet
	One-to-one support	Provided face-to-face, using floor walkers and product champions across the department

The rationale

The department has chosen an approach that leverages the scale efficiencies provided by e-learning but maintains the human touch provided by classroom training. They have also ensured that on-going support is always available via a number of dedicated channels.

This is a big change for the department but it is vital that the new systems and processes are embedded quickly. Reverting back to the paper-based system after launch is not an option. The history of poorly run Government IT programmes is on the implementation team's mind. They have decided to take an approach that makes multiple interventions available, catering for different learning styles. From the start the approach has been designed to keep people informed; and to drive change from within.

Recipe 18: Compliance training

The situation

The organisation is a large utility with a mobile workforce which rarely visits an office. The organisation needs to prove that they are compliant with health and safety procedures on an ongoing basis. Compliance with this requirement is open to external scrutiny, so non-compliance risks damage to the organisation's reputation and the possibility of fines.

The organisation feels that neither classroom training nor e-learning are practical options, given the geographic spread of the workforce and patchy access to PCs.

The strategy

The organisation has adopted a simple structured instruction strategy, applied using an innovative combination of learning media.

The blend

Elements	Methods	Media
Processes and procedures	Recorded audio, including scenarios designed to make employees think about how they would handle particular situations and to provide important information	Audio CD
	Self-study materials to capture answers and provide further information	Workbooks (employees are asked to bring these with them to the subsequent meeting with their manager for review)
Motivation	Management briefings, used to provide high-level information and check understanding	Face-to-face sessions

Elements	Methods	Media
Testing for compliance	Individual assessment	A telephone-based assessment with a set of randomly-selected questions. Employees call in from any telephone, key in their unique identification and complete the proof of learning. Results are stored in a web-based database

The rationale

It is important that the company can prove compliance and that it can renew employee accreditation, quickly and efficiently. The combination of audio CD and workbook provides a simple way to provide engaging self-study learning. The telephone-based assessment provides an innovative, automated way to check and record understanding, without the need for computers. Importantly, the management sessions provide support and a channel for issues and concerns to be resolved.

Recipe 19: Graduate trainee scheme

The situation

The organisation is a large multinational supplier of soft and alcoholic drinks, with offices, production and distribution facilities throughout the world.

The need is for a regular injection of new management talent, with the knowledge and all-round experience of the business needed to fill a wide variety of future international management positions.

The audience for each year's programme consists of around 30 graduates, typically under 25 years of age, from many different countries but all with good English language ability. The trainees are highly-motivated, independent learners, from a variety of academic backgrounds. Computer literacy is extremely good and most are already regular users of Web 2.0 technologies.

Every trainee will be provided with a laptop and will have access to good bandwidth. Training facilities are available in every major country, but budget constraints and environmental considerations dictate that travel should be kept to a minimum.

The strategy

The programme will be designed with an emphasis on guided discovery and exploration, reflecting the capability of the trainees to learn independently to a large extent.

The blend

Elements	Methods	Media
Preparation	Meeting with local mentor	Face-to-face
	Visit to facilities in home country	N/A
	Reading about the company	Online on intranet
	Viewing recorded video material about the company	Online on intranet

Elements	Methods	Media
	Networking (to make initial contact with other trainees)	Social networking site on intranet
Induction	Ice-breaking activity	Classroom in central location
	Presentations to introduce the programme	As above
	Group problem-solving activities to develop group cohesiveness	As above
	Facilitated discussion	As above
Work experience (in three blocks throughout the year)	Trainee works in three different capacities, providing an insight to different aspects of the business' operations	On-job, locally or in other regional facilities
Group projects (in parallel with the above)	Group projects and assignments to develop international business understanding	Virtual learning environment to support all activities
		Forums for discussion around projects
		Wiki to facilitate collaborative content development
Ongoing review and communication	Networking amongst the group	Social networking site and Skype
	Ongoing contact with tutor	Email and Skype
	Ongoing support from mentor	Face-to-face
	Reflective activity	Trainees each maintain their own blog and comment on each other's blogs
	Monthly seminars with presentations from key figures in the business	Web conferencing

Elements	Methods	Media
Conclusion of the programme	Presentations by trainees to members of senior management	Classroom in central location
	Review and discussion	As above

The rationale

The face-to-face element at the beginning of the programme allows the group to develop as an integrated learning community and establishes the international nature of the programme. The concluding session is necessary to celebrate the success of the programme and provide visibility of the progress trainees have made.

A wide variety of online tools are used to help tutors to monitor trainees' progress and to allow the group to continue to work together during the middle part of the programme, without the need for more travel.

The project work and monthly seminars provide an ongoing stream of new ideas and issues for exploration, in parallel with work experience at the coalface.

Recipe 20: European Computer Driving License

The situation

The organisation is a large National Health Service Trust, with many thousands of staff working in admin, general practice, clinics and hospitals.

The need is to ensure a uniformly high level of computer literacy as the Trust seeks to computerise more and more aspects of its day-to-day operations. The European Computer Driving License (ECDL) is an internationally-recognised qualification which assesses a computer user's ability to work with common applications such as web browsers, email clients, word processors, spreadsheets, presentation aids and databases.

The target population for the programme extends to all personnel across the organisation, with the aim to secure 70 percent ECDL attainment over a three-year period. Employees differ widely in their existing computer skills and in their attitude to computers generally.

Only a small proportion of employees has access to their own PC at work, although many have PCs at home. Computer classrooms are available at the Trust's training centre. Budget and trainer availability make it impractical for all employees to have continuous tutor support throughout the programme.

The strategy

Because many of the target population have little prior knowledge of computers and many will be dependent learners, the strategy will be one of structured instruction, albeit with a great deal of flexibility for those who wish to learn more independently.

The blend

Elements	Methods	Media
Preparation	Optional group session to provide an overview of the course and explain the options available	Computer classroom
	Activities to familiarise new users with basic PC operations	As above
	Individual reading of course overview material, as an alternative to the above	Online on intranet
Delivery	A series of workbooks, each covering a different PC application, providing instruction and activities that use the application itself	Web-based materials accessed via Learning Management System (LMS), including movies demonstrating common tasks
	Self-assessments	Online quizzes accessed via LMS, with scores recorded
Support	Tutorial support for learners experiencing difficulties	Learners with low confidence can undertake their self-study in a computer classroom with tutor support where needed
		Those learning remotely can obtain tutor support through instant messaging

Elements	Methods	Media
Assessment (learners can skip straight to this stage for any modules in which they feel sufficiently confident)	Invigilated assessments for each module	Online assessment in computer classroom with invigilator present

The rationale

This design provides support only where it is most needed. Those already PC-literate can make quick progress if they wish, while those with low confidence can call on face-to-face support as needed. Access to the computer classroom is unlikely to be an obstacle, as the Trust operates in a relatively small geographical area. Online delivery allows those who want to work from home to access all the materials freely.

To ensure that the identity of all those taking the ECDL assessments can be authenticated, these must take place in an invigilated environment, i.e. face-to-face.

Recipe 21: Drugs and alcohol policy

The situation

The organisation is a budget airline operating primarily out of the UK. The airline wishes to formalise its policy on the use of drugs and alcohol at work, not only for flight crew, but across the airline as a whole.

The airline wants its employees to better understand the effects on the body of drugs and alcohol, as well as to know the details of the new policy. Employees also need to be aware of how to respond if they encounter other employees abusing the policy. In addition, managers need to able to deal with incidents should they occur strictly in accordance with the new policy.

The target audience consists of approximately 100 managers and all 1,200 other employees.

The strategy

The strategy for both managers and other employees is essentially one of structured instruction. Because managers need to know how to handle incidents when they occur and are also required to brief their employees, the programme is structured so that managers are trained first.

The blend

Elements	Methods	Media
Managers only: Delivery	Interactive self-study materials with integrated quiz – as for all employees (see below)	Web-based materials accessed over intranet via the Learning Management System (LMS)
	Group instruction to provide an overview of management procedures	Face-to-face in classroom
	Discussion of likely issues	As above
	Role-play of incident handling	As above
Managers only: Support	Reference materials	Intranet site
	Ongoing support	HR telephone help desk
Other employees: Preparation	Team briefing by manager to cover main reasons for the policy and key elements	Face-to-face if practical, otherwise by email
	Video dramatisations of two to three scenarios demonstrating the importance of appropriate use of drugs and alcohol	Shown as part of face-to-face briefing if practical, otherwise streamed from intranet
	Discussion to debrief the videos	As part of face-to-face briefing if practical, otherwise an interactive comments facility on intranet
Other employees: Delivery	Interactive self-study materials with integrated quiz – compulsory for all employees	Web-based materials accessed over intranet via the LMS; the LMS records usage and results

Elements	Methods	Media
Other employees: Support	Reference materials	Leaflet handed out at team briefings
		Intranet site with FAQ and forum
	Support for those with confidential queries	Contact by any means with manager
		Confidential telephone help line for those not wishing to talk to their manager

The rationale

The blend for the management training element includes the same self-study component that will later be used for other employees. This ensures that managers know exactly what their employees will be told and are well prepared for their own classroom session. The classroom component is needed to provide plenty of opportunity for discussion and role play.

The employee training is designed primarily for flexibility, because of the wide variety of working arrangements and the geographic distribution of employees. Where possible employees will attend a face-to-face team briefing to ensure they understand the importance of the new policy and have the opportunity to ask initial questions. Online self-study is a practical and flexible way of subsequently delivering the training and monitoring throughput. A facility for confidential support is essential to address the needs of employees who have existing drug or alcohol issues.

Recipe 22: Maintenance of aero engines

The situation

The organisation is a manufacturer of jet engines for commercial aircraft, with customers around the world. The manufacturer needs to provide training for their customers' own engineering staff in the maintenance of a new series of engines that is about to be launched.

The audience for this training consists of engineers who have experience of working with earlier series of engines from this and other manufacturers. The new series incorporates a wide range of technological innovations which make this training more than just a routine exercise. The engineers are typically computer-literate and comfortable with the use of computers within a learning context, although their primary experience of training will have been classroom-based.

The manufacturer has an extremely well-fitted training centre in their home country and customers are used to travelling to this centre to attend lengthy classroom courses. However, there is increasing demand from a number of key customers to reduce the travel and cost commitment associated with this training, so more of their staff can obtain the training they need and in a more flexible manner.

The strategy

Because the audience is experienced, the training programme can employ a wider range of strategies: pre-work can be simple exposition; the delivery of important new concepts through structured instruction; familiarity with the new engine through exploration; and practice in troubleshooting through guided discovery.

The blend

Elements	Methods	Media
Preparation	Reading material providing background information on the new engine series	Online PDF files for download and local printing if required
	Video documentary telling the story of the design and development of the new engine series	Online streaming from secure Internet site, with DVD access as an alternative
Delivery – classroom option	Group instruction to cover essential concepts and principles	Computer classroom, using the same visual aids as the online option (see below)
	Familiarisation with the new engines	Visit to see the engines
		Computer classroom: 3D models for individual exploration
	Troubleshooting practice	Computer classroom: worked example, instructor-led; then individual practice using computer-based scenarios
	Review and discussion	Computer classroom, instructor-led

Elements	Methods	Media
Delivery – online option	Interactive self-study to cover essential concepts and principles	Online web-based materials from secure Internet site, with CD-ROM as alternative
	Familiarisation with the new engines	3D models for individual exploration, accessed as above
	Troubleshooting practice	Worked example, followed by multiple opportunities for individual practice using computer-based scenarios, accessed as above
	Review and discussion	Access to online tutor using instant messaging and/or email
		Discussion forum for all trainees, moderated by online tutor
Support	Ongoing reference to information about the new engine series and troubleshooting guides	Online web-based materials from secure Internet site, including 3D models used as part of delivery (see above)

The rationale

The provision of two alternative modes of delivery allows the manufacturer to respond to the preferences and expectations of different customers. Duplication of effort is reduced because both options utilise many of the same visual aids and e-learning software. This is particularly true for the 3D models, which will be expensive to produce and need, therefore, to be exploited as much as possible.

Recipe 23: Car sales training

The situation

The organisation is a manufacturer of prestige, high performance cars with a large network of dealers. The manufacturer needs to provide sales training to support the launch of a highly-innovative new range of fuel efficient vehicles with extremely low carbon emissions. They need to be sure that salespeople are fully aware of the unique features and benefits of the new range and understand the customer profile at which the range is directed.

The audience consists of approximately 800 salespeople widely distributed around the country, most of whom are highly experienced and very knowledgeable. More than 90 percent of the audience is male and extremely enthusiastic about cars. They find it easiest to relate to 'petrol heads' like themselves, customers who have been attracted to the company's high performance profile. On the whole, the salespeople are computer-literate, but have been used to receiving their training at lengthy face-to-face events which also serve as 'jollies.'

Every salesperson has access to their own computer, with ample bandwidth. It is the nature of the job that there are quiet times when there is sufficient peace and quiet for learning activities. The manufacturer has well-equipped training facilities in each region, along with examples of each new model, before it has been officially released.

The strategy

The blend uses a variety of strategies at different stages: familiarisation with the new range is accomplished by simple exposition; the core sales training element uses guided discovery, with the aid of a series of scenarios in a virtual showroom; ongoing skill development is achieved through structured instruction on a one-to-one basis with the local sales manager.

The blend

Elements	Methods	Media
Familiarisation	Reading: in-depth background on the new range	Online web-based materials
	Watching video: interviews with product designers; previews of TV ads	As above
Sales training	Simulated sales scenarios in which learners respond to typical customer enquiries; decisions taken by learners influence the outcome of the sales interviews; many alternative scenarios are provided to allow learners to have as much practice as they need	Online 3D simulation for individual use, set in a virtual showroom; linked to learning management system to record usage and completion
Motivational session	On successful completion of sales training, learners attend live motivational session, with opportunities to see and drive the new vehicles	Face-to-face at regional centres
Follow-up	Coaching from dealership sales manager in line with briefing notes supplied	Face-to-face in local dealership; results are collated online through the learning management system

The rationale

Simple, high-quality web-based materials are more than adequate for initial familiarisation, given that the audience is already experienced in sales and technically knowledgeable. The choice of a virtual world for simulated sales practice cuts down on the time spent away at face-to-face events and makes use of the quiet times that salespeople experience. It also allows for much more individual practice than can be accomplished in a group training setting.

The motivational session acts as a reward for successful completion of the training, allowing salespeople to network with each other and see the vehicles close up. The coaching from the sales manager ensures that the training is followed through on-the-job.

Recipe 24: Personal safety training

The situation

The organisation is a charitable trust which specialises in providing support to employees who are likely to experience aggressive behaviour in the course of their work. The trust is hoping to enhance its current training programme by working with communities of learners over a more protracted period than is possible with a simple classroom event.

The audience is diverse, including health workers, teaching staff, transport workers and local authority employees. Typically, those attending personal safety courses have had no previous training and are extremely motivated to learn. Around 2,500 people require training each year.

The majority of learners have access to computers in one way or another, whether at work, in local colleges or libraries, or at home. Most are also sufficiently IT-literate. The new training programme will address the needs of this group, as the existing classroom-only option will continue to be made available for those who prefer it.

The strategy

As most learners are complete novices in this area, the predominant strategy will be structured instruction, although the design will also include elements of guided discovery and exploration.

The blend

Elements	Methods	Media
Introductory work	Group session to introduce the course	Teleconference
	Reading to cover basic concepts	Web-based materials, accessible from Virtual Learning Environment (VLE)
	Video material including dramatised scenes and interviews with those who have experienced aggressive behaviour at work	Web-based materials as above (also available as a DVD for those with lower bandwidth)
	Questionnaires and reflective exercises	Web-based materials
	Facilitated group discussions to debrief the above	Teleconferences backed up by discussion forums
Practical workshop	Group instruction to introduce the body language and verbal skills needed to control potentially aggressive situations	Face-to-face, with the aid of video material on DVD
	Demonstrations of the skills	As above
	Role-plays	Face-to-face in small groups
Follow-up	Learners complete individual action plans	Web-based materials on VLE
	Ongoing discussion of issues arising as learners implement action plan	Discussion forums
	Wind-up group session	Teleconference

The rationale

The decision to use a VLE as a basis for course materials and discussions is a key one, as this encourages the group to see themselves as a mutually-supportive learning community and to regard the course as an ongoing process rather than a one-off event.

The course depends on a face-to-face workshop, because there is no other realistic way to practise the interpersonal skills element of the course.

Teleconferencing is used in preference to web conferencing, as this is an easier technology to set up and use, and does not depend on students having access to a broadband connection and a headset.

Recipe 25: Major incident training

The situation

The organisations are the fire, policy and ambulance services for a major city area. The requirement is to improve the co-ordination of the three services when responding to major incidents such as motorway pile-ups, train crashes, fires and possible terrorist attacks.

The audience consists of highly-trained operatives in each of the three services, including those responsible for directing activities. Generally speaking they are motivated to improve the response to major incidents, but possibly a little defensive about the role played by their own service.

The training departments of the three services are agreed that it is not practical to run authentic exercises in real-life settings, as the disruption to the general public would be unacceptable. Computer simulations are a possibility but operatives do not typically have easy access to PCs.

The strategy

The strategy relies heavily on guided discovery using a series of simulated scenarios. These provide the opportunity for operatives to learn from their successes and failures in order to make continuous improvements in their performance.

The blend

Elements	Methods	Media
Pre-briefing	Group briefing conducted separately for each service	Face-to-face
	Video to show real incidents, including interviews with participants	As above, using DVD
	Individual reading of operating procedures and guidelines	Printed material

Elements	Methods	Media
Simulation	Real-time, multi-player scenarios in authentic settings with in-game tutor feedback	Multi-player virtual world in which scenarios can be acted out using VOIP (Voice Over Internet Protocol) and 3D avatars; these run on laptops incorporated into mobile IT facilities, located at the HQ sites of the three services
De-briefing	Group de-briefing conducted separately for each service	Face-to-face
(These three steps repeat until the performance objectives have been accomplished)		

The rationale

The use of multi-player virtual worlds for the simulations allows for repeated practice without disruption to the general public. The pre and post briefings are conducted face-to-face as this is the only practical option given limited access to PCs.

Recipe 26: Product training for salespeople

The situation

The organisation is a multinational software development company, which in recent years has become more heavily involved in the gaming and advertising markets. There is significant competition in these markets and the technology advances quickly, necessitating constant up-skilling and fresh product knowledge.

The learners are young, media-savvy salespeople, selling advertising space and products. They have high expectations and limited time, while their primary focus will always be on hitting their targets.

The challenge here is to persuade them to increase their sales of email marketing products. These are high revenue earners for the company but, amongst sales people, there is limited product knowledge and a fear of moving away from 'tried and tested' marketing solutions.

A complication comes from the fact that different markets have different product ranges. However, a single training solution is required and the high level of market competition requires delivery of the solution in minimum time.

The strategy

The solution provides learners and trainers alike with a series of structured interventions to work with, although these are flexible and can be adapted by individuals to suit their needs. The essence of the training is to practise skills and share ideas, while building on a defined set of products.

The blend

Elements	Methods	Media
Background knowledge and practice	Having acquired a basic product understanding, the learner navigates through conversations and meetings with clients to begin practising their skills	e-Learning with video excerpts Automated email informing the learner of the next steps
Coaching	Following a group question and answer session the learner, as part of a team, is asked to present a proposal to a client by the end of the week	Conference call with SME and facilitator – learners pose their questions about the product and the programme The client brief distributed to the learners
Skills development	In a simulated client interaction, the learner looks at how the products fit into the wider product range and how to support the client after the sale	e-Learning with video excerpts Automated email informing the learner of the next steps
Preparation	At this point the teams develop their pitches, building on what the client has said and what they've learned so far	Group discussion – can be done in the classroom, virtual classroom or conference call

Elements	Methods	Media
Application	The teams present their solutions to a panel. Afterwards, the teams come together and find out who made the best pitch and has been awarded the contract. More importantly, they find out exactly why the winning team was successful through detailed facilitator feedback	Virtual or real classroom with subject expert and facilitator Immediate and three-month questionnaires – these could be paper-based or be taken online. Learners are asked if there are any gaps in information and what the impact of the training has been on their ability to sell the product

The rationale

The five elements are spread out over a week to create momentum, while a variety of methods and media are employed to maintain interest. Comprehensive facilitation notes and market-driven Q&A guides enable consistency of delivery across the globe and remove the need for highly-trained trainers, whilst concurrently enabling the programme to be tailored to regional needs.

Team work, taking place in parallel with self-study and facilitated expert sessions, allow informal and formal, individual and group, learning as well as social opportunities.

Learners have choices to make about the aspects of the products they explore as well as control over the time they spend on the training. Nevertheless, they need to take part in group activities, thus ensuring a minimum level of involvement for time-poor participants while supporting corporate goals.

Above all, each element is designed to come as close as possible to real-life activities and problems.

Recipe 27: Telecommunications induction

The situation

The organisation is a multinational telecommunications company with offices in around 50 cities worldwide. All new starters currently attend a two-day induction workshop. The first day deals with company-wide information and includes site tours and video messages from senior staff as well as key information about facilities, resources and processes. The second day is job-specific training, carried out in small groups.

The company has identified two key problems with the existing induction programme. Firstly, there is currently a high turnover of staff, which suggests that new starters are not integrating well. Secondly, the two-day programme, which often needs to be repeated for absentees, in every office across the world, consumes a lot of time and money which could potentially be used more efficiently.

The requirement is therefore to create a unifying induction programme, which will create a sense of community amongst staff across the globe and communicate key, company-wide messages more quickly and conveniently than the existing workshop. Due to the variety of job roles, all new starters must still undergo one day of face-to-face, job-specific induction training.

The strategy

The organisation decided on a programme centred on structured instruction to ensure the key messages are communicated effectively, with additional elements of exploration and social interaction designed to combat the high turnover rate.

The blend

Elements	Methods	Media
Welcome message	Welcome message from the head of the organisation, introducing the company's vision and the induction process	Podcast

Elements	Methods	Media
Networking	A facility for meeting colleagues, asking questions and becoming familiar with the company culture	Online social networking site
Key messages	Introduction to the company history, strategy and ambitions, along with important information relating to health and safety, HR and career development	30-minute e-learning course, including a 3D modelling element allowing a virtual site tour
Integration	Social gathering to allow learners to meet colleagues in a relaxed setting outside the office	Face-to-face social gathering

The rationale

The new, four-stage induction programme combines formal and informal learning with social opportunities to ensure that the dual objectives of reducing company time spent on inductions, while still fostering a familial environment are met.

The only mandatory training is the online element, which communicates all the key messages about the company and its culture, facilities and processes. This ensures a minimum level of knowledge and competency but offers the learner further opportunities to extend their induction outside company time.

To further encourage this interaction with other employees, the induction programme begins before the learner officially starts work. The welcome message podcast is the first stage in an ongoing integration and support programme. The social networking site, which can be used long after starting work, encourages new starters to seek advice and information from their peers rather than their line manager (again, reducing the need to answer these questions during company time). The social gathering goes a long way towards enhancing a feeling of integration and combating high staff turnover.

The combination of formal learning, informal learning and social interaction means that information is available in a format to suit every learner and provides an ongoing support system beyond the formal online training course and job-specific induction workshop.

Recipe 28: Negotiation skills for salespeople

The situation

The organisation is a multinational software development company. The requirement is for comprehensive and ongoing training for their sales force in negotiation skills.

These sales people are young and media-savvy with high levels of motivation to hit targets and develop professionally. Despite being self-motivated, the learners have limited time and are constantly on the move.

The organisation has been running a very successful and popular three-day negotiation skills workshop for some years. However, there is a need for a high-profile refresher resource that encourages learners to keep reminding themselves of the basic techniques and applying them throughout their career. The organisation is keen that any refresher elements are presented as an extension of the workshop and that all parts of the solution form a 'family' of learning resources.

The strategy

The organisation has chosen to adopt a mix of learning strategies to fulfil the different elements of the requirement. Structured instruction will be used to deep-dive into the skills and processes involved in negotiation. A mixture of exploration and exposition will then be used to practise and embed the learning. Finally, an element of guided discovery will be used to build motivation and as a refresher. This will be in the format of a serious game in order to engage learners to the extent that they are willing to spend their free time participating.

The blend

Elements	Methods	Media
Soft skills	Three-day, skills-based workshop, with participants engaging in a number of mock negotiations over the three days; these case-plays are recorded for subsequent evaluation and discussion	Classroom with video facilities
Processes and procedures	The same workshop provides a wealth of tips and techniques for use at various stages of negotiation and these are structured into an eight-step process for clarity	Classroom
Review, practice and application	The learner is provided with a brief, high-level review of the content that was covered at the workshop in the form of an introductory video from the workshop facilitator and 10 minutes of interactive self-study. They then practise and apply the skills from the workshop by participating in a series of simulated negotiations	60-minute, scenario based e-learning course with video
Ongoing performance support / reinforcement	A serious game whereby the learners have to negotiate a number of situations within a highly-developed scenario	Serious game, online

The rationale

The centrepiece of the solution is the three-day workshop which provides invaluable opportunity for group discussion and personalised feedback, and face-to-face soft-skill development.

Following the workshop, the e-learning allows learners to review and refresh what was learned at the workshop as and when they require it. An introductory video from the workshop facilitator directly links the e-learning to the classroom-based activities and provides recommendations on how to get the best from the online elements. A series of assessed, multipath scenarios with a strong, game-like element provides a useful, challenging and engaging way to practise and develop the skills they learned at the workshop.

For this audience of young, time-pressured sales people, the serious game provides the incentive needed to encourage them to learn outside company time. The combination of learning substance and fun, delivered through a rich-media vehicle, is the ideal motivator for this audience, providing easily-accessible, ongoing performance support and reinforcement.

Section five
Appendices

Appendix 1: Responding to the situation

This table examines the implications of particular situational variables when making your choice from the four main training strategies described by Clark and Whittrock (2001) and when choosing the learning medium. Where several alternative strategies are listed, the author's preference is listed first. In practice, choice of strategy is also likely to be influenced by the training and learning culture in your organisation. For more information on the four training strategies, see Appendix 2.

Situational variable	Suggested training strategy	Implications for selection of learning media
Nature of the learning		
Knowledge of facts and concepts	Structured instruction Exposition (with care to avoid overload) Exploration (where there is no need for the learner to demonstrate particular learning)	
Knowledge and understanding of processes and principles	Guided discovery (e.g. simulations, games, case studies, projects, assignments, discussion, coaching) Structured instruction Exposition (with care to avoid overload) Exploration (where there is no need for the learner to demonstrate particular learning)	

Situational variable	Suggested training strategy	Implications for selection of learning media
Knowledge and understanding of rules and procedures	Structured instruction Exposition (with care to avoid overload) Exploration (where there is no need for the learner to demonstrate particular learning)	
Cognitive (problem-solving) skills	Structured instruction (e.g. drill and practice) Guided discovery (e.g. simulations, games, case studies, projects, assignments, discussion, coaching)	
Social (interpersonal) skills	Structured instruction (e.g. role plays) Guided discovery (e.g. simulations, games)	The training will normally require a face-to-face element to allow for realistic practice of the skills
Psychomotor (physical) skills	Structured instruction (one-to-one or group) Guided discovery (e.g. using simulators, coached practice, etc)	Practice of these skills requires an authentic setting, typically face-to-face, although some psychomotor tasks can be simulated
Attitudinal change	Guided discovery (e.g. questionnaires, case studies, simulations, role play, group discussion) Exposition (e.g. stories, personal accounts)	

Situational variable	Suggested training strategy	Implications for selection of learning media
Learner characteristics		
Learner is capable of learning independently	Learner will be comfortable with any of the strategies, but is likely to prefer exploration	
Learner is dependent on trainer for structure	Will learn best with structured instruction or guided discovery	
Learner is a novice in the subject being taught	Will learn best with structured instruction or guided discovery	Learner may benefit from face-to-face support initially
Learner is experienced in the subject being taught	Learner will be comfortable with any of the strategies, but will have a preference for more learner-centred approaches	
Learner is motivated to learn the subject	Any strategy will be appropriate	Less important to use rich media to engage the learner
Learner is not motivated to learn the subject	An element of guided discovery may help the learner to understand the importance of the topic A competitive element in structured instruction or guided discovery may motivate the learner	The use of rich media or virtual worlds may help to engage the learner

Situational variable	Suggested training strategy	Implications for selection of learning media
Practical constraints		
Learners are widely dispersed geographically		Classroom training will be more time-consuming and expensive If time zones vary widely, it will make it more difficult to organise real-time online events
Learners find it hard to allocate large blocks of time during the working day		Classroom training will be more difficult to schedule
There is only a small audience for the training		Favours media that require less design and development, otherwise the cost per head will be prohibitive
Time available to complete the training is limited		Favours media that require less design and development Favours media that deliver the required learning in the shortest time (typically modular and self-paced)
Access to computers is limited		Makes any computer-based delivery harder to accommodate
Access to suitable network connections is limited		Makes online delivery more difficult
Access to training facilities is limited		Assuming outside facilities cannot be easily rented, classroom training will be more difficult to accommodate
Trainer time is limited		Assuming outsourcing is not an option, the situation favours self-study media, which require little or no trainer involvement

Appendix 2: Training strategies and supporting methods

This table provides examples of training methods likely to be supportive of each of the four main training strategies described by Clark and Whittrock (2001). Typically a selection of these methods will be required to fulfil the strategy. Note that different strategies could be employed at different stages in a learning intervention. See Appendix 3 for examples of media options applicable to each training method.

Strategy	Supporting training methods
Exposition (training by telling) Learning model: Learner as a sponge or spectator; absorbs information provided	Prescribed reading Viewing recorded video material Listening to recorded audio material Viewing slide presentations with recorded narration Group lecture / presentation Subject matter support (Q&A) Individual test / assessment Performance support / reference
Structured instruction Learning model: Learner as a builder of associations through responses to carefully planned stimuli	Interactive self-study lesson / tutorial Group or one-to-one instruction Subject matter support (Q&A) Facilitated group discussion Individual drill and practice Individual practice (observed by trainer and/or other learners) Individual test / assessment Group or one-to-one progress review Performance support / reference

Strategy	Supporting training methods
Guided discovery Learning model: Learner as a problem solver	Group ice-breaking activity Questionnaire / inventory Individual or group planning activity Individual or group problem-solving activity / exercise (e.g. a case study, problem-solving task, scenario) Individual or group game or simulation Individual or group project or assignment Individual or group visit Individual or group reflection activity Individual work experience Facilitated group discussion One-to-one coaching or mentoring Group or one-to-one progress review Exploration of a 3D space / object Collaborative content development
Exploration Learning model: Learner as an active builder of knowledge	Individual exploration / research Reading Viewing recorded video material Listening to recorded audio material Viewing slide presentations with recorded narration Questionnaire / inventory Performance support / reference Subject matter support (Q&A) Unfacilitated group discussion (e.g. using a bulletin board / blogs) Attendance at lectures / presentations Exploration of a 3D space / object Collaborative content development Networking

Appendix 3: Training methods and options for their delivery

This table lists a selection of training methods and provides examples of media that could be used for their delivery. Do not be constrained by this list as you will no doubt be able to come up with additional methods and further ways in which the methods listed here can be realised. For an analysis of the comparative benefits of the various media options, see Appendix 4.

Method	Media options
INDIVIDUAL	
Reading	Books / other printed materials Workbooks Documents contained on removable computer media (CD-ROMs, etc.) Web pages (Internet or intranet) Downloadable documents (PDF, Word, PowerPoint, etc.)
Viewing recorded video material	Downloadable video files for playback on computers and personal media players ('vodcasts') Playback on computer from removable computer media (CD-ROMs, etc.) Streamed delivery from the Internet or intranet Playback on VCRs, DVD players, etc. using removable media Broadcast transmission (TV) Playback during face-to-face events Playback during a virtual classroom session

Method	Media options
Listening to recorded audio material	Downloadable files in MP3 and other compressed audio formats for playback on computers and personal media players ('podcasts')
	Playback on computer from removable computer media (CD-ROMs, etc.)
	Streamed delivery from the Internet or intranet
	Playback on dedicated audio players (hi-fi's, car stereos, etc.) from removable media
	Broadcast transmission (radio)
	Playback during face-to-face events
	Playback during a virtual classroom session
Viewing slide presentations with recorded narration	On CD-ROM / other removable media
	Online web-based delivery
Exploration of a 3D space / object	3D models embedded in a downloadable PDF file
	On CD-ROM / other removable media
	Single-user virtual worlds
Planning activity	Unsupported activity (requires no media)
	Exercise in workbook
	Exercise on CD-ROM / other removable media
	Exercise online (Internet or intranet)
Reflection activity	Unsupported activity (requires no media)
	Exercise in workbook
	Exercise online (Internet or intranet)

Method	Media options
	Exercise on CD-ROM / other removable media
	Maintaining a blog
Exploration / research	Unsupported activity (requires no media)
	Resources could include all media listed above under 'prescribed reading', 'viewing recorded video material' and 'listening to recorded audio material'
	Attendance at seminars or conferences
Questionnaire / survey / inventory (including 360 degree feedback methods)	Paper-based activity
	Online activity (Internet or intranet)
Interactive self-study lesson / tutorial	In workbook
	On CD-ROM / other removable media
	Online web-based delivery (Internet or intranet)
Problem-solving activity or exercise (e.g. a case study, problem-solving task, scenario)	On CD-ROM / other removable media
	Online web-based delivery (Internet or intranet)
	Live online lab (for IT training)
Game or simulation	On CD-ROM / removable media
	Online web-based delivery (Internet or intranet)
	Use of dedicated simulator
	Single-user virtual worlds
Drill and practice	Exercise in workbook
	On CD-ROM / other removable media
	Online delivery (Internet or intranet)

Method	Media options
Test / assessment	Exercise in workbook
	On CD-ROM / other removable media
	Online delivery (Internet or intranet)
	Telephone (using recorded audio-based questions, with voice or key input)
Assignment / project	Unsupported activity (requires no media)
	The assignment could be set up and followed up using a wide variety of media
Visit (to observe the work of others / to share experiences)	Face-to-face
	The visit could be set up using a wide variety of media
Work experience	Unsupported activity (requires no media)
Performance support / reference	Books / other printed materials
	On CD-ROM / other removable media
	The web (Internet or intranet)
	Downloadable documents (PDF, Word, PowerPoint, etc.)
ONE-TO-ONE	
Instruction	Face-to-face (on-job or off-job)
	Virtual classroom (possible but unusual)
Subject matter support (Q&A)	Face-to-face
	Email / SMS messaging
	Instant messaging
	Telephone

Method	Media options
Coaching or mentoring	Face-to-face Email / SMS messaging Instant messaging Telephone
Progress review	Face-to-face Email / SMS messaging Instant messaging Telephone
GROUP	
Ice-breaking activity	Workshop / class Forum / bulletin board Virtual classroom Text-based chat Teleconference Multi-user virtual world
Energising activity	Workshop / class Virtual classroom Text-based chat Multi-user virtual world
Lecture / presentation	Seminar / conference Workshop / class Virtual classroom / 'webinar' Multi-user virtual world Can also be recorded using a variety of media for individual access
Instruction	Workshop / class Small group (on-job) Virtual classroom Multi-user virtual world

Method	Media options
Subject matter support (Q&A)	Workshop / class Forum / bulletin board Virtual classroom Text-based chat Teleconference Multi-user virtual world
Facilitated discussion	Workshop / class Forum / bulletin board Virtual classroom Text-based chat Teleconference Multi-user virtual world
Unfacilitated discussion (e.g. for planning, sharing, reflection)	Workshop / class (as a syndicate) Forum / bulletin board Virtual classroom Text-based chat Teleconference Blogs Multi-user virtual world
Problem-solving activity / exercise (e.g. a case study, problem-solving task, scenario)	Workshop / class Forum / bulletin board Virtual classroom Multi-user virtual world
Multi-player or group game or simulation	Workshop / class Virtual classroom Online web-based delivery (Internet or intranet) Use of dedicated simulator(s) Multi-user virtual world

Method	Media options
Individual practice (observed by trainer and/or other learners)	Workshop / class Small group (on-job) Virtual classroom (possible but unusual) Multi-user virtual world
Real-world project or assignment	Unsupported activity (requires no media)
Visit (to observe the work of others / to share experiences)	Face-to-face
Progress review	Workshop / class Small group (on-job) Forum / bulletin board Virtual classroom Text-based chat Teleconference Multi-user virtual world
Networking	Social network Workshop / class Seminar / conference Multi-user virtual world Blogging
Collaborative content development	Wiki / online word processor Downloadable documents Workshop / class

Appendix 4: Comparative benefits of learning media

This table lists the principal practical and learning benefits of the most common learning media. It can be used as a reference when selecting the most appropriate medium for the delivery of a chosen learning method. For a list of learning methods and the options available for their delivery, see Appendix 3.

	Practical benefits	Learning benefits
Offline media	No requirement for a network connection	Potential for high-quality media
Books / other printed materials	Portable, easy-to-use	Potential for very high resolution text and still images
Workbook	Portable, easy-to-use	Encourages limited interactivity when used for self-study Can include still images
Video (cassette, DVD) / also broadcast TV	Can be watched at home or in a training room without the need for a PC	Potential for high quality video and audio
Audio (cassette, CD) / also broadcast radio	Can be listened to at home or in a training room without the need for a PC Can be listened to in cars or using portable music players while on the move	Potential for high quality audio
Simulator	Allows learners to develop complex skills without the need for access to the real equipment or job environment, and without risk to safety	Learners can experiment with manoeuvres that would be too risky or expensive using real equipment in the real job environment

	Practical benefits	Learning benefits
Removable computer media (CD-ROM / DVD-ROM / Memory sticks / Flash cards, etc.)	Usable on any computer or mobile device with the appropriate drive, whether or not there is a network connection No bandwidth constraints Much cheaper to replicate and less bulky than printed materials	Can contain a wide variety of digital media including text, still images, animation, audio, video, PDF files and Office documents Can contain all forms of interactive, self-study materials, including assessments, tutorials, games and simulations
Online media (via PCs, mobile devices, digital TV)	All online media benefit from the capability for remote access, eliminating the time and cost incurred in travel for learners and tutors	
Web pages	An unlimited amount of information can be made available extremely cheaply Information can be accessed from any location where a network connection is available Audio and video can be streamed to the user, obviating the need for download Learners can control when they access material and for how long	Can contain a wide variety of digital media including text, still images, animation, audio and video Can contain all forms of interactive, self-study materials, including assessments, tutorials, games and simulations

	Practical benefits	Learning benefits
	Information on learner activity and progress can be automatically stored centrally on an LMS Because the data is only stored in one place, the learner sees only the latest material	
Downloadable documents (PDF, Word, PowerPoint, etc.)	An unlimited number of documents can be made available extremely cheaply Documents can be accessed from any location where a network connection is available	Depending on their type, documents can contain a wide variety of digital media formats
Downloadable media files (audio, video, Flash movies)	An unlimited number of media files can be made available extremely cheaply The media files can be downloaded wherever a network connection is available Can be copied to portable media players for access while on the move (podcasts, etc.)	Potential for high quality video and audio Flash movies can support all forms of interactive self-study, including assessments, tutorials, games and simulations
Email / desktop alerts / SMS messaging	Because communication is asynchronous, the learner is not tied to a specific timetable	Provides a learner with asynchronous access to tutors and other learners
Instant messaging	Can achieve a quicker response than email The software informs the learner when their contacts are online	Provides a learner with real-time access to tutors and other learners, with the option of audio and video communication

	Practical benefits	Learning benefits
	VOIP (Voice Over Internet Protocol) provides an alternative to the telephone, without call charges	
Text-based chat	Easy to set up and use	Provides a learner with the opportunity for real-time collaboration with other learners
Forum / Bulletin board	Because communication is asynchronous, the learner is not tied to a specific timetable Easy to set up and use	Provides a learner with the opportunity for asynchronous collaboration with other learners Benefits those learners who do not enjoy real-time group collaboration
Blog	Because communication is asynchronous, the learner is not tied to a specific timetable Easy to set up and use	Encourages reflection Provides a learner with the opportunity for asynchronous collaboration, by adding comments to other learners' blogs and by responding to comments made on their own blogs Benefits those learners who do not enjoy real-time group collaboration
Wiki	Because communication is asynchronous, the learner is not tied to a specific timetable Easy to set up and use	Allows learners to collaborate on assignments and in creating content for use for by other learners in the future Benefits those learners who do not enjoy real-time group collaboration

	Practical benefits	Learning benefits
Virtual classroom / web conferencing	Sessions can be recorded for those who miss the live event Experts do not have to travel in order to participate, making it easier to call on experts from anywhere in the world	Provides an online alternative to the classroom for real-time, one-to-one, small group and large group communication and collaboration Includes the capacity for real-time audio and video-based communication (at the high end, as with Cisco's Telepresence, this makes the process as natural as face-to-face communication) Allows for application sharing, which can be useful for IT training
Multi-user virtual world, e.g. SecondLife	Synchronous communication allows meetings, workshops and other events to be held in the virtual world	Virtual worlds can be extremely engaging Realistic settings can be designed to provide a more authentic experience Learners can interact through their avatars (on-screen personas) anonymously if they wish
Single-user virtual world	Because communication is asynchronous, the learner is not tied to a specific timetable	Virtual worlds can be extremely engaging Realistic settings can be designed to provide a more authentic experience
Social network	Because communication is asynchronous, the learner is not tied to a specific timetable Relatively easy to set up	Allows learners to create and maintain contacts in order to find and share expertise

	Practical benefits	Learning benefits
Live online lab (for network engineers)	Avoids the need to make complex networking equipment available in the classroom	Network engineers can explore alternative configurations without risk to company networks
Telephone		
Automated, individual access	Simple and universally-available	Provides access to recorded audio information and to assessments using audio-based questions
One-to-one call	Simple and familiar technology, with which most learners will be comfortable	Allows real-time voice communication between a student and their tutor
Teleconference	As above, although requires more planning than a simple one-to-one call	Allows real-time voice communication between groups of learners and their tutor
Face-to-face	Does not depend on particular equipment, materials or connectivity	Face-to-face communication is real-time, multi-sensory and highly flexible
On-job training	Learners do not have to travel to a central training location	Learners can observe real-world behaviour and practise in an authentic setting
Workshop / class	A highly-flexible and familiar format that is relatively easy to administer	Supports a very wide variety of training methods. The trainer can augment their delivery with flip charts, whiteboards, slides, videos, models, etc. Participants can work in small groups where required Equipment (PCs, machines, etc.) can be brought into the classroom to allow demonstrations and practice

About the author

Clive Shepherd MA FCIPD FIIT FBILD MCMI

Clive Shepherd is a consultant specialising in the application of technology to education, training and employee communications. With more than 25 years of experience in this field, Clive is acknowledged as a thought leader in all aspects of e-learning and blended learning.

Clive developed his interest in interactive media at American Express in the early eighties, where he was Director of Training and Creative Services. He went on to co-found Epic, a leading content developer, in which he played a variety of management roles.

Since 1997, Clive has worked with a wide range of public and private sector organisations on the application of technology to learning and employee communications. In 2003 he received the Colin Corder Award for services to IT training, and in 2004 the award for Outstanding Contribution to the Training Industry at the World of Learning conference.

In the last few years, much of Clive's work has concentrated on the training of trainers to take an active and enthusiastic role in the implementation of e- and blended learning in their organisations.

Clive is also an active and enthusiastic designer of e-learning and blended learning interventions. His course Ten Ways to Avoid Death by PowerPoint won the prize for best generic e-learning programme at the World of Learning Awards 2004. His blended learning design for an international management development programme at Plan International won a National Training Award in 2008.

Clive's writing on e-learning can be found in his books and more than 100 published articles. He has a monthly column in e.learning age magazine and posts regularly to his blog, Clive on Learning. He is also a regular speaker at UK and international conferences.

From 2007-2011 Clive was Chair of the eLearning Network.

He now concentrates his activities on Onlignment, a consultancy firm for which he is a founding partner.

He lives in Brighton with his wife Susan. When he gets away from all things e-learning he likes to walk on the South Downs, play tennis and keep fit generally. He's also a keen musician.

Blog: http://clive-shepherd.blogspot.com

Email: clive@onlignment.com